Judith Butler: Live Theory

Also available in the *Live Theory* series from Continuum:

Judith Butler: Live Theory

Vicki Kirby

continuum

Continuum International Publishing Group

The Tower Building   80 Maiden Lane
11 York Road   Suite 704
London   New York,
SE1 7NX   NY 10038

First published 2006
Reprinted 2007

British Library Cataloguing-in-Publication Data
A catalogue record for this book is available from the British Library.

ISBN: 0-8264-6292-8 (hardback) 0-8264-6293-6 (paperback)

Library of Congress Cataloguing-in-Publication Data
A catalog record for this book is available from the Library of Congress.

Typeset by BookEns Ltd, Royston, Herts.
Printed and bound in Great Britain by
MPG Books Ltd., Bodmin, Cornwall

Contents

Preface

It is something of a platitude to acknowledge Judith Butler as one of the most prolific and influential writers in the academy today. Her work spans philosophy and contemporary theory as well as political commentary and popular culture, and its analytical complexity is well known. In the hope of capturing something of the spirit of this achievement within the confines of the series' parameters I've had to make some difficult editorial decisions regarding content and approach. I was aware that readers who might be entirely unfamiliar with this style of intellectual work would be looking for guidance and clarification. However, I was not prepared to sacrifice the intricacy of Butler's ideas to a more inclusive, yet inevitably superficial exegesis.

What follows then is a detailed engagement with a selection of the more important themes in Butler's work, a careful unpacking that aims to be accessible as well as critically provocative. It is, of course, an interested reading, one that will reveal as much about my own commitments, prejudices and understanding as it does about Butler's. However, to the best of my ability I've tried to remain faithful to the letter and intention of Butler's argument, even, or especially, where I register my criticisms.

In the interview, the reader will catch something of the breadth of Butler's work, some of the important material that couldn't be included here, as well as the directions in her forthcoming projects. But of course, it is Butler's own words that are being represented in this volume, and I can only encourage the reader to explore the challenge in these writings for herself. If Butler's work is a valuable scholarly template, it is not so much as a doxa to be affirmed and simply followed, but as an exemplary illustration of how to read critically, yet generously. As I share Butler's interest in thinking about the politics of interpretation and critique, my modest hope is that I have read Butler in a way that will underline why a critical reading practice has political and social consequences.

Acknowledgements

Research for this project was funded by a University Research Support Program Grant from the University of New South Wales.

A version of Chapter 4 first appeared as 'Poststructuralist Feminisms: Part 2' in *Telling Flesh: The Substance of the Corporeal* (New York and London: Routledge, 1997).

Dita Svelte, Demelza Marlin and Colleen Pearl have provided assistance at various stages of the project, and Anna Bennett, Heather Worth and Carol Sullivan have given helpful feedback. I would also like to thank Liz Wilson, Karen Barad and Tom Lamarre for their insight and encouragement.

For Vigo

Precarious Foundations – Subjects of Desire: Hegelian Reflections in Twentieth-Century France

In 1987 Judith Butler's first book, *Subjects of Desire: Hegelian Reflections in Twentieth-Century France*, introduced readers to many of the enduring themes that have continued to sustain her interest, and although Butler describes this first effort as 'juvenilia' its importance to her later achievement is clear.[1] As Butler herself notes, '[i]n a sense, all of my work remains within the orbit of a certain set of Hegelian questions' (1999a, xiv). In the following chapters we will see this set of questions revisited in explicit terms in *The Psychic Life of Power* (1997a), *Antigone's Claim: Kinship between Life and Death* (2000a), and in discussions with and about political theorists such as Slavoj Žižek and Ernesto Laclau. Perhaps more importantly, we will also see that the discernible signature of Butler's prolific output and contribution to a broad field of academic and activist concerns, regardless of subject matter, derives from an implicit curiosity about the political consequences of the Hegelian legacy.

However this legacy is no ordinary inheritance from an authoritative antecedent. Indeed, Butler problematizes its actual identity when she imbues the act of reading with an interpretive efficacy that can continue to change it. It is as if the text is an animate and evolving life form, or as Butler explains, 'Hegel's text is itself transformed by the particular historical interpretations it endures; indeed, the commentaries are extensions of the text, they *are* the text in its modern life' (1987a, 63). This talmudic incorporation of interpretation within the body of

Hegel's work complicates our ability to discriminate between the specific contributions of individual authors, between the meaning of what was said then as opposed to now, and between what is ancillary or derived and what is central or primary. The difficulty in determining what properly belongs where and to whom reflects the internal ambiguities of language itself and the impossibility of fixing a text in any final way. Of course, the equivocal nature of meaning and identity is not specific to the Hegelian oeuvre, yet Butler discovers something exemplary in the sense of unfinished business that Hegel's argument dramatizes. Given this, we will need to understand why Butler regards Hegel's thesis as comprehensively disorienting, and why the instability of its paradoxical structure helps to illustrate her own concerns.

Butler divides the argument in *Subjects of Desire* into four parts: (1) an extended critique of desire in Hegel's *Phenomenology of Spirit* which gives special attention to two of the most debated sections – 'The Truth of Self-Certainty' and 'Lordship and Bondage'; (2) an appraisal of the different interpretations of Hegelian desire which Alexandre Kojève and then Jean Hyppolite introduced to two generations of young French scholars;[2] (3) a discussion of Jean-Paul Sartre's yearning for a self-identical (pre-Hegelian) human subject and his reading of desire as an inevitably futile and self-deceiving force; and finally, (4) a critical assessment of the revisions of several post-Hegelian theorists, namely, Jacques Lacan, Gilles Deleuze, Jacques Derrida and Michel Foucault, who aim to achieve a more thorough subversion of the metaphysics of identity.

Given the conceptual complexity of Hegel's argument and the detail in Butler's analysis, the modest goal of this commentary is to convey something of a 'feel' for this style of thinking. Why, for example, has 'coming to terms with Hegel' been such a compelling and yet frustrated need for so many philosophers and social critics? To take us into the puzzle, Butler approvingly cites a remark made by Maurice Merleau-Ponty to emphasize Hegel's defining importance. 'One could say without paradox that to give an interpretation of Hegel is to take a position on all the philosophic, political and religious problems of our century'

(1990a, 249). The comment still resonates for Butler despite Hegel's seemingly curious insistence that history had come to an end in 1807!

But not everyone is comfortable with the spatial and temporal metaphorics of closure, finitude and constraint that Hegel seems to be offering, and many thinkers are provoked to seek a way out of its imperative logic. In his inaugural address to the Collège de France, for example, Michel Foucault grants Hegel's authority and significance but with a decidedly less appreciative nod to the master. Foucault suffers Hegel's totalizing presumptions, judging them a prohibitive obstacle rather than a fertile resource for envisaging political possibilities. '[W]hether through logic or epistemology, whether through Marx or Nietzsche, our entire epoch struggles to disengage itself from Hegel' (cited in Descombes 1982, 12). A few years prior to Foucault's observation, Jacques Derrida comments with some amusement that those who would 'undo the constraint of Hegel' can find themselves 'without seeing or knowing it, *within* the very self-evidence of Hegel one often thinks oneself unburdened of' (1985, 251). Derrida offers a salutary warning that the emancipatory impetus in readings such as Foucault's might represent a naïve recuperation of the desire for transcendence. And yet perhaps even he can be accused of wanting much the same thing when he attempts to play 'a final joke on Hegel' (Butler 1987a, 179) that could, just possibly, trump the master.

Even in these few brief comments we gain a sense that there may be no alternative route around the implications of Hegel's work, for as Butler observes of those who would avoid or correct him, 'references to a "break" with Hegel are almost always impossible, if only because Hegel has made the very notion of "breaking with" into the central tenet of his dialectic' (1987a, 183–4). And yet it is the 'self-proclaimed anachronicity of Hegel's own text' (Butler 1990a, 249), this sense that we are somehow displaced while remaining bound *within* something, that fascinates Butler, motivating her to explore the strange internal architecture of this apparent enclosure. Thus, for Butler, the aim is not so much a trumping of Hegel as it is the work of interrogating the political challenge and consequence of finding other worlds, other temporal exigencies and existential possibilities within what seem to be restrictive and oppressive determinations.

In sum then, the Hegelian dialectic is difficult to reckon with because it thrives on opposition. For example, in rejecting Hegelianism we underline its resilience, for the dialectic can accommodate all opposition and critique. Butler's aim in *Subjects of Desire* is a sustained investigation of this very point:

> Throughout my inquiry I will be concerned with the dissolution of Hegelianism as well as the peculiar forms of its insistent reemergence, its reformulation, and its inadvertent reappearance even when subject to its most vehement opposition. Indeed, we will see the degree to which opposition keeps desire alive. (1987a, 15)

The following discussion will provide a preliminary sense of what is at stake in Butler's engagement with Hegelianism and it will also introduce the reader to a mode of philosophical thought that exceeds its institutional or disciplinary definition as Philosophy proper. Although the full implications of this last point will require some familiarity with Butler's work as a whole, we can at least begin to acknowledge why Hegel's logic might appear even in the prosaic rhythms and meanings of the everyday. We will explore the ubiquity and paradoxical implications of this logic and consider why Butler might embrace it when others either struggle to emancipate themselves from it or claim to have already done so. Our primary interest then will be in the way that Butler puts Hegel to work to envisage different futures.

The puzzle of identity

Butler's *Subjects of Desire* focuses specifically on Hegel's *Phenomenology of Spirit*. Organized as a *bildungsroman*, a novel about the process of education (ex-ducare – a leading out), the *Phenomenology*'s unfolding journey elucidates the forces that enable transformation and self-discovery. Similar stories about self-recognition and moral development, stories such as John Bunyan's *Pilgrim's Progress*, Charles Dickens' *Great Expectations* or Cervantes' *Don Quixote*, are conventionally written in a specific genre that relies upon careful narrative development. However, Hegel's narrative is an unusual one as it draws upon the conventions of story-telling while at the same time disrupting the linear structure that allows the tale to progress. It is as if we are moving forward while remaining in a place which is uncannily familiar, as if we are learning more and more about something we already seem to know.

Hegel effectively disorients the reader by paying special attention to how language determines our perception of space and time. To explain this, when we read we implicitly rely on certain grammatical forms to distinguish one thing from another. For example, we use what in linguistics are termed 'shifters', words such as 'now', 'today' or 'here'. These little markers are comparatively empty but for the reader's ability to inform these 'holes' in the text with a quite specific sense of temporal and spatial relevance.[3] We also differentiate subject from predicate to produce a temporal sequence, or order of events, that allows us to ascribe locality and to separate things spatially. Importantly, this also enables us to distinguish action from passivity and to infer an explanatory direction or sense of causality from the sentence's internal arrangement.

However, Hegel's writing style tends to disorient and confuse the reader, causing us to pause and consider how a narrative actually functions. As a consequence Hegel's sentence structure begins to weigh awkwardly, disabling the easy flow of meaning and making us aware of the inherent ambiguity and mediating influence of language. The identities of subjects and objects in Hegel's account interpenetrate and become blurred, and we inevitably lose our bearings and read sentences again and again to recover our place. We even become confused about the identity of the subject whose journey towards self-consciousness Hegel chronicles: we are increasingly unsure if the subject encountered along the way, a subject who seems to be another quite separate individual from the main protagonist, is actually one and the same. Is this a story about *inter*-subjective or *intra*-subjective recognition, or more provocatively, are these separate processes? For example, in the first encounter of self-consciousness, an encounter which appears to involve two subjects, their mutual recognition is described by Hegel as a 'spiritual unity in its duplication' (1807/1977, 111). Hegel explains:

> Self-consciousness is faced by another self-consciousness; it has come *out of itself*. This has a twofold significance: first, it has lost itself, for it finds itself as an *other* being; secondly, in doing so it has superseded the other, for it does not see the other as an essential being, but in the other sees its own self. (1807/1977, 111)

The ambiguity is maintained by Hegel, as each time one subject seems to differentiate itself from the other and assume a separate identity the narrative switches perspective and the difference collapses: are there two subjects here, or just one, caught in the movement of its own reflection?

> Each sees the *other* do the same as it does; each does itself what it demands of the other, and therefore also does what it does only in so far as the other does the same. Action by one side only would be useless because what is to happen can only be brought about by both.
> Thus the action has a double significance not only because it is directed against itself as well as against the other, but also because it is indivisibly the action of one as well as of the other. (1807/1977, 112)

Reading the *Phenomenology* is a little like being in a carnival mirror-maze where myriad distorting reflections turn identity into something elusive and dispersed. We are presented with an imago whose recognition involves an ambiguous and fluid field of reflections with no stable reference point to stop or steady the process. Without a fixed ground the reader's identity is also 'subjected' to this disorientation and we begin to perceive that even reading is a form of recognition that must constantly undo itself through movement. This dense interplay of association constitutes the very stuff of identity, where apparently separate units or events are actually referentially complicit with each other, indeed, they somehow *are* each another. For Hegel and for Butler, the operations of language exemplify this process.

In a later chapter we will devote considerable attention to the question of language and its special relevance to Butler's work and to contemporary cultural and post-structural criticism more generally. However, at this stage it is important to mention two related considerations that will advance our understanding of Hegel's enterprise. First, the signature of Hegelianism is most powerfully evident in the way the dialectic, the motor of change, is regarded as a dynamic whose operational energies are *internal* to a 'system'. In other words, the forces of change, differentiation, movement and opposition are not external assaults upon the system, forces that hail from outside it to rupture its integrity; rather, they are expressions of an essential incoherence or disjunctive reflex *within* the system. The second, related point is that Hegel uses language to exemplify this paradox because its operational complicities couple the system's self-reference, its apparent invariance, with the open-ended inventions and neologisms that change it from within. Because language is not a transparent vehicle of pre-given meanings derived from an extra-linguistic reality, language poses a question about the unifying and generative principle of systematicity itself, in all its manifestations. Once we realize that the differences that appear external to a system, differences that seem alien and 'other', represent the system's own internal reconfigurations, then we begin to appreciate why the subject of Hegel's narrative, and the processes that enable its identity, implicate subject formation and semiology.

Given this, Butler interprets Hegel's 'tortuous text' as an *enactment* of a process that *is* the subject, a subject who signifies indefinitely and whose ambiguity is never finally resolved.[4] Even the copula, that grammatical and logical predicate of existence most simply articulated in the verb 'to be', can no longer secure ontological integrity. It operates more like a node of reflexive movement, such that the being of an apparently individual thing *is* the self-involvement of the system's 'being individuated'. Butler justifies the necessity for Hegel's circuitous narrative and its constitutive importance to his argument in the following comment:

> Because Hegel's rhetoric defies our expectations of a linear and definite philosophical presentation, it initially obstructs us (no one reads Hegel quickly), but once we have reflected upon the assumptions that Hegel wants to release us from, the rhetoric initiates us into a consciousness of irreducibly multiple meanings which continuously determine each other ... In reading for multiple meanings, for plurivocity, ambiguity, and metaphor in the general sense, we experience concretely the inherent movement of dialectical thinking, the essential alteration of reality ... the human subject is never simply and immediately there. As soon as we get a grammatical indication of his location, he travels forth and becomes something different from what he was when we first got wind of it. (1987a, 19–20)

The dilemma in trying to introduce Hegel's work is that 'to begin at the beginning' is already to imply the whole conceptual apparatus of his metaphysics, for an origin will already anticipate the future that has yet to arrive. Thus, as with any identity, it seems that even the origin's identity is strangely elusive. What first appears as one discrete thing, whether a moment in time, an event, an individual subject or a specific action, can be shown to involve what today we might liken to an infinite hypertext of nested associations. Perhaps a helpful way to think about this ubiquitous, fluid, and yet at the same time, quite focused and specific sense of identity that Hegel evokes is not to think so much of hyper*links*. In other words, these are not joins that separate or connect one identifiable thing with another through extraneous attachments that may or may not be activated. Rather, for Hegel these differences are internal to any entity, the self-generating volatility that enables that entity to continue to become 'this thing' or 'this subject' – this determinate existence.

To clarify this, within a conventional understanding of relationality the separateness of things isn't called into question when dependence and historical connection are acknowledged. We are able to grant, for example, that a baby is completely dependent on its mother for its existence, while still believing that there are two individuals involved. We assume that their difference predicates the very possibility of their relationship, and that although they may be affected and changed by that relationship they will remain identifiably separate and uniquely themselves. However, Hegel's *Phenomenology* does more than demonstrate this conventional understanding of indebtedness to otherness.

For Hegel, every 'entity' incorporates the other it has yet to encounter, such that its difference from another individual subject evolves through a difference, or transformation, within itself. We can extend the mother/baby example to illustrate what Hegel might be getting at here if we take the mother's genetic 'signature' as a marker of her individual identity. This signature is interpreted as evidence that she is one particular subject *among* others. And yet although the child is also unique, in a very real sense it represents a repetition, albeit reconfigured, of the mother's script: in other words, the mother returns in/as the child. However, this would imply an infinite re-collection of identity, as the child's mother is also her own mother, that is, the newborn's grandmother, and by implication the newborn is the grandmother continuing to become herself!

We might counter the autonomy of the maternal line's reshuffled identity by saying that a radically alien script, namely that of the father, must be introduced from the outside to make this inventive repetition possible. And yet this would assume that the father's identity is somehow pure and outside maternal recuperation, as if he has no mother of his own. But even leaving this criticism aside, we can come at the problem from a different tack if we *begin* with the identity of the human genome itself.[5] With the genetic *system* as our subject we can see that although every individual's personal genetic signature is completely different from another's, these differences don't confound the genome's identity: they exemplify it. In other words, difference isn't 'the other' of identity but rather an expression of its own process of becoming (other). If we think about identity in this way we can see that there are no real isolates (autonomous individuals) in this example, for the genome's identity *is* the differential of its in-finite re-combination. In a sense then, just as the genome will always 'know' and 'be' its different manifestations, Hegel's journeying subject embodies the Life of an Everyman; an epigenesis that is constantly evolving into itself.

Difference and negation

Hegel's term for the structural unrest of the dialectic is *aufhebung*, a German word that conjures three seemingly distinct yet simultaneous operations. In English, the word 'sublation' is often used to capture the movement of *aufhebung*, a movement which Butler explains 'cancels, preserves, and transcends the apparent differences it interrelates' (1987a, 41). It is a process that implies directional or purposive progression towards a higher unity, a synthesis that effects a transmutation of opposites into a new and presumably more knowing form of self-consciousness. However, if we are already wary of reading Hegel's narrative in strictly linear terms, that is, as the subject's developmental maturation towards the telos of complete knowledge and self-understanding, we might reasonably assume that the implicit progressivism of the dialectical structure is similarly deceptive.

What makes the dialectical movement of the 'via negativa' difficult to follow is that it surreptitiously abandons the conventions of logical sense. Butler encourages us not to assume that Hegel is simply irrational in this, for as she notes, 'the question is not what logical sense can be made of negation in Hegel, but how the very use of negation in Hegel calls into question our understanding of logical relations' (1999a, x). To unpack the building blocks of this process, the dialectic appears to retain the dual structure of opposition by affirming the truth of the negative and its destructive force, and yet at the same time it annihilates the negative's logical purchase as an *enduring* truth by affirming its opposite. The slippery description of this process involves a sort of perspectival ambiguity, for every 'yes' must also imply a negative assertion, an implicit rejection. Instead of two separate forces then, each one pitted against the other, the dialectic is perhaps better understood as the torsional energies within a system that make it 'work' or move.

There are still a lot of questions here, but what should be getting clearer is that if every 'entity' or 'moment' is constitutively caught up with what it would oppose or separate itself from, and here we are thinking about negativity as such, then the supersession or transcendence of the negative, the 'negation of negation', actually enables, and indeed is, the negative's transmogrified reappearance. We have already noted something of this ironic logic in the suggestion that the subject's identity becomes/is all that it encounters: in other words, an individual whom I perceive to be other to me is more than a separate person, an independent self, possessed of an identity that is 'not mine'. Although appearances may suggest otherwise, Hegel argues that an encounter with an Other is always a form of self-encounter. Thus, identity is precarious and paradoxical for Hegel because its essential being is an alien possession ('I am an other'). This means that the identity of the negative which enables and indeed *is* this process is the interrogative force of identity's constant interruption of itself; the internal disquiet of relentless reinvention. Perhaps the happy logic in the expression 'The king is dead! Long live the king!' captures something of its paradox.

Negativity usually implies a sense of 'no', and it can carry such meanings as prohibition, absence, lack or failure, finality, limitation and death. Unfortunately, it is this associational matrix of restriction and conformity that critics often bring to Hegel's work, assuming that the negative is quite straightforwardly an oppositional force, and that the system which enables it is a fixed and finite totality of normative regulation and interdiction with inevitable outcomes. However, Butler's reading of 'the labour of the negative' lingers over the political implications of its transformative potential:

> Although Hegel is often categorized as the philosopher of totality, of systematic completeness and self-sufficient autonomy, it is not clear that the metaphysical totality he defends is a finite system. Indeed, the abiding paradox of Hegel's metaphysics seems to consist in the openness of this ostensibly all-inclusive system. For a metaphysics to be simultaneously complete and infinite means that infinity must be included in the system itself, but "inclusion" as a spatial relation is a poor way of describing the relationship ...
> (Butler 1987a, 13)

Butler finds in negation the possibility of regeneration and human freedom and she endeavours to recover these more hopeful signs even from the annihilating lessons that would reduce human life to nothingness. As we see here, Hegel's negative is so resiliently renegade that it can even vanquish death by giving itself to it ... totally: '... the life of Spirit is not the life that shrinks from death and keeps itself untouched by devastation, but rather the life that endures it and maintains itself in it. It wins its truth only when, in utter dismemberment, it finds itself' (1807/1977, 19).

In sum then, and to make a point whose political significance will become apparent in later discussion, oppositional logic is insistent and resourceful, a masquerade of inventive guises. The negative is something of a feint, a counterfeit, a ruse, indeed something that compromises any simple discrimination between the truth and the lie, the original and the copy, yes and no, here and there, now and then. As we saw in the previous discussion, even the difference between the One and the Other seems to collapse in Hegel's understanding of self-encounter, where intra-subjectivity and inter-subjectivity cohere. To imagine a world where the discriminations that allow us to identify and reason become so entangled that the meanings and justifications for a way of life are made precarious would be an unhappy prospect for many. But for those whose lives are already precarious and existentially fragile?

Butler's social conscience motivates her to read philosophy in terms of such questions, for it is clear that many people, whether through economic and geographic circumstance or through the ongoing discriminations of sexual and racial difference, are forced to survive and even endorse 'the way it is'. However the rhythms and logics of our world are also fuzzy and inconsistent: they never simply repeat themselves. Indeed, what is the perverse nature of change (the negative) that its manifestations can even appear as a resistance to change, or even be alive in the most conservative institutions and foundational structures of a society? How might the dialectic's errancy offer us a way to rethink our approach to political analysis and action? This is the task that Butler sets herself.

Desire

As the title of Butler's exploration of the *Phenomenology* makes clear, the organizational engine of the book, its true subject, is

Desire. It is 'the action of supersession itself' (Butler: 1987a, 43), the interrogative force of life that enables the re-vision of being in knowing. Yet Hegel doesn't name it as such until 'The Truth of Sense Certainty', the fourth section of the *Phenomenology*, and Butler asks a very important question about its sudden emergence at this juncture of the story. She queries how the force which drives the whole of the *Phenomenology* could simply 'appear' at a certain time: wouldn't Desire have to precede its own emergence and be there from the beginning? Butler explains the conundrum: 'Desire *appears*, but the moment of appearance is not necessarily the initial moment of its efficacy. In a sense, nothing comes into existence *ex nihilo* for Hegel; everything comes into explicit form from a potential or implicit state; indeed, everything has, in a sense, been there all along' (1987a, 24).

Although Butler's clarification is important it isn't meant to displace the significance of Hegel's decision to delay Desire's entry in the *Phenomenology*. In fact, the delay is especially interesting if we consider that we would normally tend to associate desire with primordial urges, with the passions and the unruly animal drives of the body that precede cognition and circumspection; in other words, we would make a simple separation between body and mind and assume that the former precedes the latter. However, as the logic that associates 'the primordial' with 'woman, native, other' has been closely analysed and contested in cultural criticism, Hegel's delayed introduction of Desire is salutary. After all, we might 'naturally' expect Desire to come first. Yet the timing and content of such assumptions goes awry when Hegel elides Desire's insatiable hunger for the world with an omnivorous curiosity that *is* the process of reflection and self-consciousness: 'self-consciousness is *Desire* in general' (Hegel: 1807/1977, 105). By explaining curiosity in corporeal terms, the binary separation of body from mind, and by association, Nature from Culture, is significantly destabilized. For if Nature is not 'given' as an original reference point against which the evolved difference of cognition can be identified and measured, then what will anchor those hierarchical oppositions whose logic presumes it: woman/man, primitive (ignorant, black)/civilized (enlightened, white), passionate (subjective)/logical (objective), and so on.

Rather than assume that the body is the passive precondition for cognition's later arrival, cognition emerges as the body's essential medium. Butler underlines the point: 'If desires are essentially philosophical, then we reason in our most spontaneous yearnings' (1987a, 2). Yet for many philosophers desire is something that must be put aside or overcome if reason is to be preserved.[6] Desire is considered dangerous because the urgency of corporeal needs can confuse the truth with what we want it to be, thereby making a disinterested perspective impossible.[7]

However, if the movement of Desire/Self-consciousness can be likened to the vagaries of Life, as Hegel seems to suggest, then the temporal breaks in the narrative that fall under different headings are somewhat misleading. Whether we think of Hegel's subject as Desire, Self-consciousness, Language or Life (the differences blur), the subject is not made up of an amalgam, or inclusion, of different 'parts'. Rather, these 'parts' are particular modes or 'moments' of the subject's own being (itself): they are manifestations of the internal torsions, the reflexive curiosity which the subject has for itself in its difference.

Given this sense that the subject's internal convulsions can't really be broken down into separate moments of emerging complexity (for the subject is always/already itself in every aspect of its difference), we might wonder what grounds the comparative evaluation of any one thing over and against another. As we have already noted, there is an implicit denigration of 'otherness' that sexualizes and racializes difference as something that is lacking. Women, for example, are commonly regarded as more emotional than men and therefore closer to Nature: this purported inability to control themselves is then taken as evidence of their incapacity for abstract and logical thought. But why is alterity aligned with the corporeal, and why does its purported primitivism attach to certain actions, capacities and subject formations rather than to others?

In 'Lordship and Bondage', the most famous section of the *Phenomenology*, Butler explores this question's political resonance in explicit terms. As she explains:

... the drama of recognition and labor must be seen as permutations of desire; indeed, what we witness in this chapter is the gradual specification of desire: self-consciousness as desire *in particular*. The notion of desire loses its reified character as an abstract universal, and becomes situated in terms of an embodied identity. (1987a, 43)

A staging of the mirror experience when one self-consciousness, or what appears initially as *the* One and only self-consciousness, is confronted by another self-consciousness, the One is displaced in the recognition that 'its own essential principle [is] embodied *elsewhere*' (Butler: 1987a, 48). Prior to this experience the subject consumed all that it encountered, actively vanquishing otherness, or so it thought. It failed to realize that its ability to recognize and ingest otherness and to make otherness like itself meant that otherness *was* itself. Consequently, it now feels threatened by this Other self-consciousness whose apparent independence and freedom could exact the same murderous price. Hegel describes the ambiguous displacements in this struggle:

> It must supersede this otherness of itself. This is the supersession of the first ambiguity, and is therefore itself a second ambiguity. First, it must proceed to supersede the *other* independent being in order thereby to become certain of *itself* as the essential being; secondly, in so doing it proceeds to supersede its *own* self, for this other is itself. (1807/1977, 111)

There is a subtle connection of otherness to corporeal vulnerability and need here, as if the annihilation of the body of the other might secure absolute freedom. As Butler explains, this 'anti-corporeal erotic ... endeavors to prove in vain that the body is the ultimate limit to freedom, rather than its necessary ground and mediation' (1987a, 52). With the realization that the desire to annihilate threatens all of life and therefore any possibility of recognition, domination, or 'the effort to annihilate within the context of life' (1987a, 52), becomes an acceptable compromise.

The dramatization of this trauma and its broader political ramifications are poignantly clear in Butler's summation:

Terror gives rise to dissociation. The lord cannot deny his body through suicide, so he proceeds *to embody his denial*. This internalization of an intentional relation, i.e., its transformation into a reflexive one, itself engenders a new intentional one: the reflexive project of disembodiment becomes linked to the domination of the Other. The lord cannot get rid of the body once and for all – this was the lesson of the life and death struggle. And yet he retains the project of becoming a pure, disembodied "I," a freedom unfettered by particularity and determinate existence, a universal and abstract identity ... freedom does not, in the tacit view of the lord, require bodily life for its concrete expression and determination. For the lord, bodily life must be taken care of, but just as well by an Other, for the body is not part of his *own* project of identity. The lord's identity is essentially beyond the body; he gains illusory confirmation for this view by requiring the Other to *be* the body that he endeavors *not* to be. (1987a, 53)

The irony of this struggle between lord and bondsman, analysed by political theorists ever since, is captured in the complex identity of the bondsman. As a mere instrument of the master's intention, a passive conduit for his needs, the bondsman must spend himself in physical labour in order to satisfy those needs. However, as the bondsman works with the brute stuff of the material world, labouring to make it answer his own demands, he comes to appreciate the tacit independence that Nature exhibits in its very resistance to him. Although the bondsman is successful in making Nature into a thing he can use, his ability to do this involves learning *how* Nature might lend itself to his purposes. In other words, Nature's own difference from him must be an active determinant in this transformative process. Thus, the bondsman's negation of Nature is not a simple act of controlling consumption, for he is not the sole agent of the object's transformation any more than transformation is a process that simply acts on the object. Indeed, as natural objects come to reflect the internal complexity of their makers, the identifying difference between subject and object, or the original site of creative agency, is increasingly unclear.

Similarly, if we return to the political asymmetry that followed the confrontation of self-consciousness with itself we discover that the bondsman is beginning to appreciate how freedom and self-determination can emerge from dependence, whereas the apparent freedom, autonomy and privilege of the lord has translated his hubris and controlling pomposity into an inevitable dependence on the one he controls. The master is so full of himself, so impassive and hermetically sealed against the world's (his own) complexity, that he remains unwittingly ignorant and truly alienated from himself. Importantly, and as Butler reminds us, 'the gradual inversion of their initial roles offers lessons in the general structure and meaning of desire' (1987a, 56).

We are probably far enough into the duplicitous seductions of Hegel's metaphysics to appreciate that its counter-intuitive inversions can't simply be put right. The interrogative force of Hegel's argument, especially in its challenge to our understanding of 'initial conditions', means that the question of the origin is an enduring one. Butler's analytical attentions will reprise the origin for its unexamined political investments, as we will see in her constant re-reading of those attributes, subjectivities or processes thought to be originary primitives; the pure datum of Nature. But there is one implication to this mode of questioning which has yet to be acknowledged.

The 'systematic philosophy' of the *Phenomenology* is figured through the trope of 'Geist', a mysterious and evocative word whose ambiguity represents something of a quandary. Put simply, 'who' is the story's protagonist? The presumptive starting point that conflates the subject with the human subject, with ordinary and extraordinary human beings caught in the process of becoming more reflective about their constitutive fragility, seems right. However, as the involved circuitry of Hegel's systematic encounter turns any starting point or identity into a heuristic and provisional device, this should give us pause. The confusion is dramatized in the different conceits that organize the *Phenomenology*'s totalizing motive. When the subject of the narrative appears in such forms as 'Sense-Certainty', 'Perception', 'Force', the 'Concept', 'Desire', 'Life' or 'Consciousness', we tend to see these terms as personified stages of humanity's evolution towards self-consciousness. After all, as the journeying subject arrives at different 'stations' of the narrative's development, it comes to recognize these stations as transitional moments of self-encounter. Surely, if Desire is an immanent rationalism, could the subject be anything other than human?

Although Butler describes the *Phenomenology* as '[t]he philosophical cultivation of sensuousness into an all-embracing truth' (1987a, 241), a truth which is not alien to the corporeal, she is careful to insist that it is not 'ordinary experience' or 'daily life' in its seeming immediacy that Hegel evokes. For Butler, 'the "experience" of the *Phenomenology* is never devoid of philosophical appropriation; although the referent is implicitly the ordinary experience of human beings, this referent is never disclosed as outside of the philosophical language that interprets it' (1987a, 241). Butler presumes that philosophy, or human thought, mediates our perceptions of the world because the in-itself of reality can only be communicated through the technology of language. And yet the conundrum of mediation in Hegel's semiology may well be more ambiguous and capacious than Butler's clarification of its human properties acknowledges. In Hegel's account, if 'the before philosophy' is still philosophy, need we necessarily assume that this Life of Self-inquiry and interrogative movement is defined and contained by human identity?

An interesting question for us to consider is whether the intricacy of the 'system' that Hegel explores is the subject of *human* be-ing in its individual and collective expression, or Being more generally. This is a consideration we will return to in our overall assessment of Butler's aims and their achievement in her various writings. Suffice it to say here that Butler signals a preliminary warning against 'the conceptual need to delimit in advance the necessary historical conditions – the presumption of continuity, intersubjective *sens* and the human actor as a synthesizing subject' (1990a, 257), for it predetermines 'the political' and what can be asked.[8] In the following chapters, we will consider whether the radical drive in Butler's work to reconfigure the subject might, on its own cognizance, be taken further.

Chapter 2

Gender, Sexuality, Performance – Gender Trouble: Feminism and the Subversion of Identity

First published in 1990 and reissued in 1999 with a new preface, *Gender Trouble* remains Butler's best-known and most influential work to date. A germinal text for the emerging field of queer theory, the book's major contribution is its critical examination of the identity categories in sexual political debate. Butler's engagement with the problematic of identity in *Subjects of Desire* anticipates the style of argument in this, her second book. In short, Butler maintains that a commitment to identity, one which considers the content of categories such as sex, gender and sexuality to be self-evident and unambiguous, will inevitably deny the complex reality of people's lives and the impure histories of political struggle.

The main target of Butler's intervention is the heterosexism of feminism. At that time, and although the women's movement had been forced to admit the racial and economic tensions that divided women and their allegiances, the facticity of 'woman' was relatively intact as the reference point for these debates. However, feminism's heteronormativity was more awkwardly engaged, perhaps because gender and sexuality had come to imply one another. Indeed, the lesbian experience had even been generalized as a shared female erotic – something akin to the commitment, friendship and sensual familiarity that attaches to being female.[1]

Importantly, Butler's critique of what could be described as a heterosexist fundamentalism is not a simple corrective that attempts to replace one mistaken identity or perception with a more worthy or accurate one. As her aim is to acknowledge the complex forces that render *any* identity inherently unstable, Butler extends her criticisms of feminism's identity politics to contest a presumptive lesbian and gay identity that defines itself against the failures of feminism. In sum, *Gender Trouble* explores the tactical juggle that comes with admitting the provisional nature of identity, while at the same time acknowledging that identity is a political necessity with an experiential reality.

Gender Trouble is organized into three main chapters 'that effect a critical genealogy of gender categories in very different discursive domains' (1990b, xi). Chapter 1, 'Subjects of Sex/Gender/Desire', introduces the reader to the basic terms of the debate, exploring the continuities and discontinuities between these categories as well as the foundational status of 'woman' for both feminism and the sex/gender distinction. The relationship between language and power, an organizing theme for the entire book, is explored through the work of French feminist writers Monique Wittig and Luce Irigaray.

Chapter 2, 'Prohibition, Psychoanalysis, and the Production of the Heterosexual Matrix', revisits Claude Lévi-Strauss and structural accounts of social organization, interrogating the explanatory importance of the incest taboo as the default line of cultural intelligibility. Butler questions the supposed coherence of gender, the heterosexual frame which demands it and the social hierarchies it installs and legitimates. Her critique is two pronged. Deploying a psychoanalytic approach to the question of identity formation, in particular, through the work of Jacques Lacan and Joan Riviere, Butler is provided with an account of structural heteronormativity. Although an account she is clearly critical of, psychoanalysis proves useful because it acknowledges that normative identifications are imperfectly achieved, just as prohibitions are always compromised and precarious. Butler then considers psychoanalysis and the incest taboo through the lens of Michel Foucault's work on the repressive hypothesis. As Foucault's insight is that the nature of power is so thoroughly perverse that even juridical power and repression incite the law's subversion, Butler asks: '[i]s psychoanalysis an antifoundationalist inquiry that affirms the kind of sexual complexity that effectively deregulates rigid and hierarchical sexual codes, or does it maintain an unacknowledged set of assumptions about the foundations of identity that work in favor of those very hierarchies?' (1990b, xii)

Chapter 3, 'Subversive Bodily Acts', forms the final section, and together with a brief conclusion, 'From Parody to Politics', is popularly regarded as *Gender Trouble*'s signature argument. Although Butler's uneasy response to the book's enthusiastic reception was to significantly rethink performativity, this early representation, given its broad acceptance, deserves consideration. Butler also explores the body politics of Julia Kristeva in this section, bringing a Foucauldian critique to the normative investments in her representation of the maternal body. However, criticisms of Kristeva in one regard don't prevent Butler from finding subversive purchase in other aspects of her work, namely, her treatment of abjection. Similarly, the usefulness of Foucault's work on juridical power doesn't blind her to the theorist's inconsistencies, especially his 'problematic indifference to sexual difference' (1990b, xii). In sum, the organizing focus in this chapter is the production of structural asymmetry: how are individual bodies as well as the larger social body carved into regularizing grids of narrow binary possibility? Butler will develop a politics of performative resignification to challenge these normative determinations by coupling the theory and fiction of Monique Wittig with Julia Kristeva's work on abjection.

Subjects of sex/gender/desire

This chapter opens with several brief citations whose collective consequence represents a significant assault on the very foundations of sexual identity and desire:

> One is not born a woman, but rather becomes one.
> – Simone de Beauvoir
> Strictly speaking, "women" cannot be said to exist.
> – Julia Kristeva
> Woman does not have a sex.
> – Luce Irigaray

> The deployment of sexuality ... established this notion of sex.
> – Michel Foucault
> The category of sex is the political category that founds society as
> heterosexual.
> – Monique Wittig
>
> (1990b, 1)

To situate these assertions and explain what is at stake in their transgressive economy Butler begins with a discussion of 'woman', a category whose substantive referent in sexual anatomy seemed to provide natural support for feminism's earliest struggles toward emancipation. It was as if being a woman was a fact whose simple self-evidence could unite ethnic, class and racial differences and even transcend cross-cultural experience. Coupled with the global identity of 'woman' were similarly sweeping assumptions about men, in particular, that all women suffered the oppression of a universal system of male domination, a patriarchy whose exploitative advantage for males was clear.

Although not in direct disagreement with this, the growing appreciation that cultural factors were a powerful force in determining how biology was interpreted certainly complicated the picture. Beauvoir's provocative claim that 'woman' is a cultural artefact significantly displaced biology's organizing relevance for feminism, just as anthropological and historical research discounted sexual anatomy as an explanation of gender diversity. As Butler explains: 'Originally intended to dispute the biology-is-destiny formulation, the distinction between sex and gender serves the argument that whatever biological intractability sex appears to have, gender is culturally constructed: hence, gender is neither the causal result of sex nor as seemingly fixed as sex' (1990b, 6).

Given the apparent disjunction between sex and gender we should not be surprised by 'the fragmentation within feminism and the paradoxical opposition to feminism from "women" whom feminism claims to represent ...' (1990b, 4). Butler's point here is that identity politics disavows the violent exclusions, the normative demands and compromises which any definitional unity exacts. In other words, the lived reality of 'women' may incorporate such different experiences that the very existence of a shared identity becomes tenuous.

However, Butler takes the argument further, underlining the scandalous implications of separating sex from gender when she asks if '*man* and *masculine* might just as easily signify a female body as a male one, and *woman* and *feminine* a male body as easily as a female one' (1990b, 6). Butler justifies her question by returning to Beauvoir's rejection of biological determinism, noting '[t]here is nothing in her account that guarantees that the "one" who becomes a woman is necessarily female' (1990b, 8). And yet even in this last suggestion – indeed, in the very terms of its expression – there is a sense that corporeal reference, the substantial fact of anatomical sex, precedes or restrains the multiple possibilities and meanings of a *later* disruption.

This enduring and explanatory reliance on the purportedly given, dimorphic materiality of anatomical sex, even within arguments that would separate sex from gender, leads Butler to ask: 'If the immutable character of sex is contested, perhaps this construct called "sex" is as culturally constructed as gender; indeed, perhaps it was always already gender, with the consequence that the distinction between sex and gender turns out to be no distinction at all' (1990b, 7). Butler's interest is in the culture of 'sex' and its genealogy: how does 'sex' come to signify a pre-cultural, passive and immutable anatomical substance (body) which precedes gender interpretation (cognition/mind)? In other words, if the dichotomy 'sex is to nature as gender is to culture' is actually an internal differential within culture itself, then what structures generate these oppositional and politically inflected differences?

Central to Butler's argument is a conviction that culture is capable of producing ontological (ways of being) and epistemo-logical (ways of knowing) frames of reference which are so powerful that they congeal into the apparent invariance and irreducibility of material reality. Indeed, for Butler, we are subjected to/through the weight of these material truths and live them as defining parameters of identity. To explain and contest the political implications of these regimes of meaning, regimes which can be so subtle that their sexualized and sexualizing logic goes entirely unnoticed, Butler turns her attention to an analysis of language.

In *Gender Trouble*, language is both an overarching template of binary regulation, a structural differential, as well as a discursive configuration that orders information into normative patterns and practices of intelligibility and legitimacy. Feminist Luce Irigaray analyses these structures closely and discovers a masculinist economy in the very grain of signification. Within the functioning 'machinery' of the sign's tiny particles, signifier (perception/body) and signified (concept/mind), as well as in the structural motor of the sign's substitutability, presence (identity) versus absence (difference), Irigaray finds a binary logic which mirrors the identity formation of male privilege: reason over emotion, mind over matter, culture over nature, phallic presence versus feminine lack. A simple illustration will explain this economy. If we consider the binary opposition of a figure/ground we can see that the two terms do not possess equivalent value. The self-evidence of the figure stands out against a ground which is its negative shadow: put simply, the ground could be described as 'something' which doesn't figure or count because it lacks presence. Conventionally, the ground is read as no*thing*, as if it doesn't have any palpable significance. However, a closer look discerns that the figure's apparent *self*-definition and autonomy are actually engendered by the ground which 'figures it forth'.

Irigaray's argument is that the binary structuration of language produces its valuations through a sexualizing economy that casts 'woman' as improper – the primordial ground against which the male subject is defined. Consequently, woman is aligned with 'otherness', 'the body', 'irrationality' and 'the animal', and all of these concepts seem *naturally* to conjure one another. The sense of an original inadequacy is again evident in woman's sexual morphology, for it is represented as an absence, or latent readiness for the phallus/child, an anatomy that requires male reference to give it meaning and purpose. For French feminist and many post-structural thinkers, the internal logic of language is described as phallogocentric because it conflates all signs of complexity, civilization and intellection with the masculine, and primordial simplicity and corporeal animality with the feminine. It also interprets these differences politically, as if the hierarchy which their comparative value installs is logical and inevitable. Irigaray responds by insisting on the transgressive positivity of otherness, arguing that the multiple manifestations of 'this sex which is not one'[2] will always elude masculinist representations that define her as lacking. For Irigaray then, 'women constitute the *unrepresentable*' (Butler 1990b, 9) because they exceed their negative assignment as man's denigrated inversion.

And yet despite Irigaray's valuable insights into the political nature of language, Butler baulks at her theory's globalizing pretensions:

> The effort to *include* 'Other' cultures as variegated amplifications of a global phallogocentrism constitutes an appropriative act that risks a repetition of the self-aggrandizing gesture of phallogocentrism, colonizing under the sign of the same those differences that might otherwise call that totalizing concept into question. (1990b, 13)[3]

Butler's point is a sobering one, for if feminists can uncritically repeat and endorse the logic of these 'colonizing gestures' then the problem can't be considered 'primarily or irreducibly masculinist' (1990b, 13). Indeed, the infection between categories must threaten to confound, or certainly complicate, the rhetoric of political analysis and fault-finding altogether if the accuser is also the accused.

Given the slippery problem that Butler uncovers here, the desire for a stable reference point that will adjudicate these ambiguities is inevitable and powerful. Irigaray seems to find it in a place outside, or before, the instrumental determinations of language which render woman's difference unintelligible. But how are we to understand such appeals when the very 'matrix of intelligibility' is in question? Butler reads Irigaray's position as a critique of the substantive grammar of sex, a grammar which 'effectively masks the univocal and hegemonic discourse of the masculine, phallogocentrism, silencing the feminine as a site of subversive multiplicity' (1990b, 19). However, Irigaray's position inadvertently recuperates substantivism inasmuch as it reinstates an ontological separation between oppositional entities that rests on the difference between nature and culture. When Irigaray insists that 'woman' is outside language because language is *essentially* repressive, instrumental and therefore masculinist, this differentiation of the inside from the outside is a binary adjudication which in Irigaray's own terms can only exist *within* language. Although a reversal of woman's familiar evaluation, no real displacement or engagement with binarity as such has been undertaken: put simply, a presumptive complexity, in this case 'woman', is identified against/outside something which fails to comprehend it – namely, language and man. Given this, Irigaray is forced into the paradoxical assertion that 'woman's' transgressive perversity throws up 'signs' (which are presumably read) of a repressive failure in language which it cannot capture.

As there is only one 'proper' sex according to Irigaray, the masculine, her work on sexual difference tends to collapse the sex/gender/sexuality nexus into the man/woman question, or what is conventionally understood as the morphology of anatomical difference. A consequence of this is that questions about 'otherness' *within* the masculine, or to take another example, questions about a panoply of different sexualities, can prove awkward for this approach. In Monique Wittig's work, however, Butler discovers a very different perspective on the binary nature of sex.

Wittig's critical intervention is focused on the reproductive aims of a compulsory heterosexuality which, she argues, enlist the body's diverse pleasures and erotic impulses towards just one acceptable outcome. According to Wittig, personhood is always designated in language by a 'grammar of gender' whose division into just one of two sexes is given a functional attribute. In other words, sexual designation becomes an alibi for sexual purpose in a system of heteronormative repression. As Butler explains:

> Gender can denote a *unity* of experience, of sex, gender, and desire, only when sex can be understood in some sense to necessitate gender – where gender is a psychic and/or cultural designation of the self – and desire – where desire is heterosexual and therefore differentiates itself through an oppositional relation to that other

gender it desires. The internal coherence or unity of either gender, man or woman, thereby requires both a stable and oppositional heterosexuality. (1990b, 22)

Unlike Irigaray who assumes that the inherent masculinism of language erases the feminine, Wittig regards language as a neutral instrument that can be used to good or bad effect by a subject who makes choices. In Wittig's view then, the possibility exists that 'the mark of gender' could be dispensed with and the subject's polymorphous, non-genital pleasures given free reign. Indeed, Wittig sees evidence of this richer existential expression in the figure of 'the lesbian', a subject deemed to be 'beyond the categories of sex' (Wittig, in Butler 1990b, 19).

Although Butler acknowledges the importance of Wittig's insight into the performative function of sexual designation as a naturalization of the sensible, she criticizes Wittig's appeal to a humanist subject whose freedoms purportedly pre-exist these regulatory regimes:

> Where it seems that Wittig has subscribed to a radical project of lesbian emancipation and enforced a distinction between "lesbian" and "woman," she does this through the defense of the pregendered "person," characterized as freedom. This move not only confirms the presocial status of human freedom, but subscribes to that metaphysics of substance that is responsible for the production and naturalization of the category of sex itself. (1990b, 20)

The commitment to a 'prior ontological reality of substance and attribute' (1990b, 20) is termed the metaphysics of substance, and Butler's entire oeuvre represents a sustained criticism of its illusionary appeal. Citing Michel Haar on this point, Butler notes that '[t]he subject, the self, the individual, are just so many false concepts, since they transform into substances fictitious unities having at the start only a linguistic reality' (1990b, 21).

Following such destabilizing assaults on our conception of reality, the reader is left in something of a quandary by the end of the chapter. Butler is clearly committed to a notion that language possesses a constitutive and regulatory force which causally implicates sex/gender and sexuality. And Irigaray's explication of

masculinism and Wittig's analysis of heteronormativity illumi-
nate this causal configuration and the repressive regimes within
language which naturalize and enforce it. Given this, a question
arises about the nature of subversion: how can these prohibitive
regimes in linguistic and cultural practice be challenged if there is
no escaping them? If, as Butler suggests, we cannot return to a
time prior to their institution nor dream of finally transcending
their restrictions, then how do we envisage the possibility of
intervention or hope to measure its success? If power inhabits the
very spatial and temporal metaphorics that its overthrow requires
('beyond', 'before', 'outside', or 'after' power), in other words, if
power is coextensive with all of the strategies and transgressive
tactics that we might use to free ourselves from it, then how are
we to proceed?

This last description of power, one which casts its identity as
perverse and ubiquitous, conjures the work of Michel Foucault,
and Butler closes this chapter by underlining the crucial
importance of his work for her project. Drawing on his insights
she raises several knotty questions which contest the possibility of
a 'specifically feminine pleasure "outside" of culture' (1990b, 30),
whether located in an untrammelled prehistory or a utopian
future. As Butler sees it, the prevailing political imperative that
nostalgically refers to an edenic existence that might again be
recovered

> ... postpones the concrete and contemporary task of rethinking
> subversive possibilities for sexuality and identity *within* the terms of
> power itself. This critical task presumes, of course, that to operate
> within the matrix of power is not the same as to replicate
> uncritically relations of domination. It offers the possibility of a
> repetition of the law which is not its consolidation, but its
> displacement. (1990b, 30; emphasis added)

In the next two chapters Butler will argue that the identity of
power itself is inherently ambiguous for its apparent unity of
purpose and causal intention are always vulnerable to perverse
calculations and energies.

Prohibition, psychoanalysis and the production of the heterosexual matrix

Claude Lévi-Strauss, the French structural anthropologist, argues that universal, bifurcatory structures inform all social arrangements, symbolic representations and economic exchange. Indebted to Ferdinand de Saussure's theory of a linguistic 'system', Lévi-Strauss privileges language as the template for social analysis because it is the prototype of all cultural phenomena, its 'unconscious structures' informing and perpetuating all aspects of social life.[4] As the nature/culture distinction, a division Lévi-Strauss also describes as 'the raw and the cooked', receives special attention in his work, the implications for feminism are considerable. As we have seen, the division is sexually and politically inflected, with nature (woman, the body) construed as the mute and passive matter that waits to be interpreted, regulated, and given social shape and significance by culture (man, mind).

Nature is *for* man, the raw material that must be tamed and controlled in order to answer his purposes and desires: thus, culture is inaugurated on a founding prohibition that bars the errant force of nature and enlists it into cultural productivity. For Lévi-Strauss it is the incest taboo, an imperative with symbolic and economic purpose, which casts women as objects of exchange to be moved between patrilineal clans. As Butler describes it, 'the bride functions as a relational term between groups of men; she does not *have* an identity, and neither does she exchange one identity for another. She *reflects* masculine identity precisely through being the site of its absence' (1990b, 39).

We might wonder why it is the lot of women to function as nameless objects, married into exile from their familiar origins and made to satisfy the sexual and economic needs of strangers. Butler accuses Lévi-Strauss of answering this troubling question by confusing the outcome with a seemingly inevitable and naturalized explanation, citing his own words as evidence, 'the emergence of symbolic thought must have required that women, like words, should be things that were exchanged' (Lévi-Strauss, in Butler 1990b, 41).

However, if these structures are explored from a different

perspective then relations among men which the heterosexual exchange of women enable must also perform a homosocial function, 'the consolidation of homoerotic bonds' (1990b, 41). Butler questions Lévi-Strauss' rigid conceptualization of recipro-cal exchange between men by asking if it implicitly prohibits reciprocity between men and women, or indeed, between women themselves. Butler closes this section of her discussion with a simple statement about the efficacy of the incest prohibition and the efficacy of the negative more generally: 'That the prohibition exists in no way suggests that it works' (1990b, 42).

Continuing her exploration of reciprocity, prohibition and identity, Butler turns her attentions to the work of Jacques Lacan, the French psychoanalyst who brought Sigmund Freud's work into conversation with Saussurean linguistics. And just as we saw in Lévi-Strauss' conflation of structural privilege with maleness, the 'proper' subject (that is, the self or ego, 'the one supposed to know') is necessarily male. Yet things are not as they seem in Lacan's theory, for the respective identities of both men and women are implicated and therefore compromised, just as what counts as knowledge involves an inevitable self-deception.

Butler explains that subject formation begins with the original enfolding of the mother/child relationship, yet this sensual involvement confounds the elements that a relationship normally requires, namely, two *separate* individuals. Following Jacques Lacan, Butler argues that the pre-individuated experience which the child has with the maternal body is lived as an auto-erotic pleasure, a merging with/in 'itself'. Importantly, there is no mother, no self before the child learns to identify, or differentiate itself from (m)otherness. According to Lacan, the origins of life remain blurred and entangled until the acquisition of language, which allows the subject to assume an autonomy and self-possession through linguistic markers, such as the personal pronoun, 'I'. Thus, language comes to 're-present' this originary plenitude (the Real, or 'lack of lack') as a world of social significations within whose binary valuations, ordered meanings, prescriptions and prohibitions the child must find its place.

Although this cultural cipher, termed the Symbolic Order by Lacan, forges ways of perceiving and being recognized in terms of the paternal law, the very identity and privilege of the masculine subject remain tenuous. Butler's explanation of the organizational importance of the Phallus in determining sexual difference makes this clear:

> For "women" to be the Phallus means, then, to reflect the power of the Phallus, to signify that power, to "embody" the Phallus, to supply the site to which it penetrates, and to signify the Phallus through "being" its Other, its absence, its lack, the dialectical confirmation of its identity. By claiming that the Other that lacks the Phallus is the one who *is* the Phallus, Lacan clearly suggests that power is wielded by this feminine position of not-having, that the masculine subject who "has" the Phallus requires this Other to confirm and, hence, be the Phallus in its "extended" sense. (1990b, 44)

The resonance with Hegel's master/slave dialectic is clearly evident in this description. Man's self-sufficiency and autonomy are predicated on a primary repression of his actual dependency and desire for the maternal body, a repression subsequently reconfigured in the conflation of woman with corporeal primordiality – she becomes *the* sex, *the* body. However, if what grounds Man's self-definition is illusory, we should not be surprised that Lacan regards relations between the sexes as a comedic play of appearances. But where does this leave feminism as it tries to contest the demands of phallogocentric privilege? In other words, how might the revelation that gender ontology is a fictional appearance be deployed to disrupt or challenge the very 'realizing' effects of masculine power?

Interestingly, Butler finds something critically useful in the very ambiguity and irresolution of Lacanian subject formation, and she is certainly not content to reject it. For example, she notes that masquerade itself is much more than it seems; much more than a compliant 'putting on', or mirroring, of patriarchal desires. After all, if feminist and lesbian subject formations are also outcomes of this performative process, then the lack of a proper referent implies that *all* identity formation is a mismeasure, a misfit. Against Butler's interpretation of masquerade as a play of possibility – a constitutive ambiguity that renders all identity improper – feminists such as Irigaray argue that masquerade covers over an *essential* femininity, a femininity whose repression in patriarchal discourse smothers its specificity, rendering it unrepresentable. '[T]he masquerade ... is what women do ... in order to participate in man's desire, but at the cost of giving up their own' (Irigaray, in Butler 1990b, 47).

Butler teases out some of these troubling differences through Joan Riviere's 'Womanliness as a Masquerade' (1986), an essay in which Riviere tries to explain the reasons behind the disjunction between biological sex and the 'characteristics, desires, and "orientations"' of certain people, especially those 'intermediate types' who 'plainly display strong features of the other sex' (Riviere in Butler, 1990b, 50). Butler notes that the presumption of a coherent correlation between sex/sexuality and gender is a perfect illustration of Wittig's insight into the heteronormative functionalism that underpins conceptualizations of sex. And yet Riviere's determination of this 'misfit' involves an explanation which effectively denaturalizes the very typologies that anchor her diagnosis, making any reference point suspect. The irony then is that while her argument takes the heterosexual matrix as its unquestioned departure point, her insistence, for example, that 'genuine womanliness and the "masquerade" ... are the same thing' (Riviere in Butler, 1990b, 53) subverts any appeal to a natural sexual identity.

Similarly, Riviere's appreciation that identity, even when apparently 'normal', may well express 'an interplay of conflicts', an unconscious strategy for maintaining or preserving something which might otherwise be lost, acknowledges the fraught dimension of subject formation. When Riviere surmises that femininity might be 'taken on' by a woman whose unconscious motivation is to hide her rivalry with men and thereby avoid the punitive consequences, she undercuts any simple adequation between certain attributes and behaviours and what they must mean. And yet, Butler makes us aware of the heteronormative investments that restrict Riviere's own interpretation of such 'conflicts'. When Riviere explains, for example, that a female who 'wishes for masculinity' is motivated by a competitive aggression to be acknowledged as a proper subject in public life and the rage of being excluded from it, she offers an important feminist insight. And yet her inability to even consider that the woman's rivalry with men/the father might involve an active homosexual desire for the mother/women goes unremarked.

Butler finds further evidence of the involved and ambiguous nature of gender identity in Freud's essay 'Mourning and Melancholia' (1917) and 'The Ego and the Id' (1923). Freud argued that mourning is the incipient structure of the ego whereby the loss of a love object, felt as the loss of the self, is 'managed' by incorporating the identity and/or the attributes of the other. The ego is thus a corporate memorial, a 'precipitate of abandoned object-cathexes ... it contains the history of those object-choices' (Freud, in Butler 1990b, 58). Butler explains that in the case of a prohibited heterosexual bond the object is denied, 'but not the modality of desire' (1990b, 58–9). However, in the case of a homosexual bond, both the object and the modality of desire must be renounced such that both 'become subject to the internalizing strategies of melancholia' (1990b, 59). The implications of Freud's argument are especially provocative when applied to questions of gender formation and the incest taboo.

Crucial to Freud's understanding of how the incest taboo actually works is the need to explain the boy's repudiation of the mother, his primary love object. The conventional interpretation of the boy's identification with the father rests on the fear of castration if his rivalry with the father continues. This heteronormative explanation is significantly complicated, however, when Freud concedes that perhaps an incipient bisexuality informs the child's ambivalence towards the parents. Butler argues that the boy is actually required to make two choices; an object choice between the mother or the father, and a choice of sexual disposition between masculine or feminine. Of course, the threat of castration becomes more ambiguous in a culture which denigrates and 'feminizes' the homosexual as an improper man. Given this, Butler muses in regard to the boy's rejection of the mother, 'do we construe the punishing father as a rival or as an object of desire who forbids himself as such?' The important point here is that this fraught constellation of sexual dispositions and object choices 'becomes the founding moment of what Freud calls gender "consolidation"' (1990b, 59). And yet the messiness of this 'consolidation' is even more apparent if we question the departure point for any analysis of sex/gender/sexuality, even those which concede the ambivalence of its categories. For in all seriousness, how is the true identity of a feminine or masculine sexual disposition established in the first place?

Interestingly, even Freud found this question impossible to answer and Butler uses his confusion to underline its irresolvable implications. Yet despite Butler's appreciation that even initial conditions are impure and involved, certain aspects of her argument presume an originary coherence. For example, when Butler comments that '[t]he resolution of the Oedipal complex affects gender identification through not only the incest taboo, but, *prior to that*, the taboo against homosexuality' (1990b, 63; emphasis added) she posits an identity that pre-exists its formation. By uncritically assuming a temporal development whereby primordial conditions (and identities) are only *later* interrupted, prohibited and transformed by culture's dictates, Butler seems to sacrifice the more persuasive and radical provocations that her argument has established; indeed, it might be said that she falls prey to the same naïve foundationalism that she criticizes in Wittig.

Despite this lapse, Butler does succeed in explaining why the most unsettling and therefore politically important aspect of the formation of sexual identity is that there is never a *pure* determination. After all, if the desire for the mother is a desire for her desire, then the mother's sexed identity as 'woman' is essentially riven with identifications/desires of/for others from the start. Indeed, precisely 'who' the mother is must remain just as undecidable as any assumption that her sexual disposition can be readily determined from the sex of her partner, same or opposite, as these discriminations can have no absolute grounding. While Butler's argument, in the main, makes us aware of such complexities, contesting the distillation of subjectivity into mutually exclusive categories and destabilizing the identity politics that any appeal to initial conditions installs, we must ask why her work inadvertently recuperates these normative categories and in ways that remain problematic for her thesis.

To continue this question, if we are persuaded that the integrity of identity is fraught from the start, then we are surely forced to wonder why the notions of 'prohibition' and 'preservation' which Freud uses to explain melancholia, and which Butler also relies upon, are not as compromised as the identities they are meant to censor or incorporate. For what can the loss of some*one* mean, in any absolute sense, if the subject was always a corporate collectivity, a 'bank' of different and constantly shifting investments? The clear discrimination which the term 'loss' retrospectively produces, as if the subject was possessed of an integrity which is only later sundered, is a point Butler makes in a different context yet fails to appreciate here. However, if we maintain the critical leverage in Butler's argument then the presumption that the process of melancholia is inaugurated by the loss/prohibition of a same-sex love object is surely problematic. If the 'original' love object was always a confused fabrication, drawn from an alienness with/in the child and, more generally, from the complex sociality which the mother instantiates (and this includes masculinity), then her identity was never simply 'same' or 'other', nor was it 'present' in a way that could be 'lost'. We will recall Butler's criticisms of Irigaray which contested the archeological conceit of a buried feminine, covered over by a masculine, Symbolic order that displaces and evacuates woman's truth. How different is Butler's own notion of power (as repression) and sexual difference (as an oppositional identity) when she insists that an intolerant culture 'must effectively displace and conceal that preheterosexual history in favor of one that consecrates a seamless heterosexuality' (1990b, 72)?

At the end of her discussion of what have been structuralist analyses of subject formation Butler again acknowledges the importance of Foucault, a theorist who 'argues on behalf of a productive law without the postulation of an original desire' (1990b, 72). And yet as we have already seen, she will continue to recuperate a repressive notion of power and a primordial sense of identity and desire without acknowledging the wavering in her position. Her concluding remarks to this section underline the thesis she struggles to maintain, namely, that it is from *within* the play of power/signification that new political possibilities emerge:

The bisexuality that is said to be "outside" the Symbolic and that serves as the locus of subversion is, in fact, a construction within the terms of that constitutive discourse, the construction of an "outside" that is nevertheless fully "inside," not a possibility beyond culture, but a concrete cultural possibility that is refused and redescribed as impossible. What remains "unthinkable" and "unsayable" within the terms of an existing cultural form is not necessarily what is excluded from the matrix of intelligibility within that form; on the contrary, it is the marginalized, not the excluded, the cultural possibility that calls for dread or, minimally, the loss of sanctions. (1990b, 77)

Subversive bodily acts

Although the concept of 'performativity' developed in this section undergoes significant transformation in *Bodies that Matter* and later in *Excitable Speech*, this earlier manifestation remains an influential contribution to the difficult question of social change. Here, Butler aims to develop a politics of subversion and she begins with a consideration of Julia Kristeva's work.

Kristeva contests the assumption in Lacanian psychoanalysis that the Symbolic order, the system of cultural determinations and prohibitions through which the child is 'subjected', is as coherent and effective as it seems. For Lacan, language acquisition is the exemplary process of acculturation, a process which severs the child's symbiotic merger with the mother and allows individuation to occur. As we have seen, the Symbolic order which cuts and divides the world into purportedly autonomous, independent and legible entities is also described as the paternal or phallic order because it aligns the unified, speaking subject with the self-definition and presence of the masculine body. And yet as Butler has already explained, inasmuch as woman figures *as* the phallus, the phallus and penis are incommensurate. With masculinity strangely compromised we might extrapolate from this that perhaps the Symbolic order, or the linguistic machinery of meaning making, is similarly fraught with an internal *in*coherence.

In *Revolution in Poetic Language* (1984) and *Desire in Language* (1980), Kristeva argues that the original corporeal energies or drives, those chaotic sensations and impulses which animate the body's raw materials, are never simply repressed by the structuring demands of a culture's symbolic economy. Although language is regarded as the systematic organization of significance, Kristeva draws 'a necessary causal relation between the heterogeneity of drives and the plurivocal possibilities of poetic language' (1990b, 81). Consequently, 'language' is not a univocal practice with fixed meaning for Kristeva, but one whose perverse energies remain evident and irrepressible in the ambiguities and condensations of poetry. This visceral, somatic sense of communicative implication Kristeva terms 'the semiotic', and she locates it in the symbiotic dependency and continuity of the mother/child relation. Thus, the language of the maternal/primordial body is an archaeological foundation according to Kristeva, and one whose dangerous energies and impulses continually threaten to disrupt the coherence of the paternal order. As Butler concisely describes these 'two modalities of language':

> In its Symbolic mode, language rests upon a severance of the relation of maternal dependency, whereby it becomes abstract (abstract*ed* from the materiality of language) and univocal; this is most apparent in quantitative or purely formal reasoning. In its semiotic mode, language is engaged in a poetic recovery of the maternal body, that diffuse materiality that resists all discrete and univocal signification. (1990b, 82–3)

For Kristeva, the space of 'the maternal body' prefigures the division between subject and object which logic requires and desire presumes, conjuring instead the libidinal impulses of an untrammelled *jouissance*.

However, in this agonistic schema of hegemonic repression and enduring resistance, an opposition whereby the 'forces of civilization' must stand ever vigilant against a more primitive and corrupting energy, the semiotic is inevitably doomed to failure because culture demands that a sense of coherence and individual autonomy prevail. Butler makes us aware of the troubling aspects of this reading when she notes that Kristeva elides the semiotic with a prediscursive homosexuality, a feminine confusion with/in the maternal body which borders on psychosis.

Denied a proper place within the Symbolic order Kristeva deems that the girl's original homosexual desire can only achieve sanctioned displacement in the maternal function and the supposedly transgressive energies of various art practices. Outside this narrow recourse, the girl's very femaleness will preserve the maternal to some extent by preventing a complete separation, but it will take the form of a sustained melancholy, a denied loss wherein female identity will be elided with negation; a lack that can't be articulated.

Butler begins her critique of this bleak and prescriptive view of subject formation and sexuality by underlining Kristeva's rigid obedience to structuralist assumptions about identity and prohibition:

> Kristeva accepts the assumption that culture is equivalent to the Symbolic, that the Symbolic is fully subsumed under the "Law of the Father," and that the only modes of nonpsychotic activity are those which participate in the Symbolic to some extent. Her strategic task, then, is neither to replace the Symbolic with the semiotic nor to establish the semiotic as a rival cultural possibility, but rather to validate those experiences within the Symbolic that permit a manifestation of the borders which divide the Symbolic from the semiotic. (1990b, 85)

Unfortunately, an inevitable consequence of Kristeva's commitment to making heterosexuality prerequisite to culture is that lesbianism must be deemed a failed sexuality, 'a site of fusion, self-loss, and psychosis' (1990b, 87).

Butler queries Kristeva's need to preserve the integrity of the Symbolic by designating the lesbian as *necessarily* 'outside Culture', caught in the expression of a regressive libidinal energy that is illegitimate and incoherent by dint of its prescribed abjection. Similarly and more broadly, the corporeal, the primitive, the Oriental, and even multiplicity and heterogeneity more generally become an external compass for Kristeva, a natural 'outside' against which the unity of the Symbolic can be located, defined and kept intact.

As Butler's political aim is the *cultural* subversion of normative identity formations, she contests Kristeva's appeal to 'a biological archaism which operates according to a natural and "prepaternal" causality' (1990b, 90), a causality which pre-exists culture. For if the alien status and make-up of 'the other' cannot be contested because its ontological difference is naturally abject, in other words, if 'the other' is beyond or before the very power of cultural practices to make a difference, then any attempt at subversion will be futile. Given this, Butler asks how those natural energies of the body which purportedly prefigure signification and culture can be comprehended and comparatively evaluated if the semiotic is truly outside signification. Committed to using Kristeva's argument rather than merely diagnosing its heterosexist and paternalistic implications, Butler notes that 'perhaps her [Kristeva's] argument could be recast within an even more encompassing framework: What cultural configuration of language, indeed, of *discourse*, generates the trope of a pre-discursive libidinal multiplicity, and for what purposes?' (1990b, 91)

In the work of Michel Foucault Butler finds an effective counter to foundationalist assumptions which understand the body as well as certain sexualities in terms of an original or fixed substrate. Foucault refuses the bifurcation of structuralism's nature/culture division, together with the causal and hierarchical logic it installs. For example, instead of accepting the facticity of biological sex as the indisputable 'given' that explains various social and political discriminations, Foucault reverses this logic by arguing that what we understand as 'sex' is already a cultural effect. In *The History of Sexuality, Volume I: An Introduction* he notes:

> We must not make the mistake of thinking that sex is an autonomous agency which secondarily produces manifold effects of sexuality over the entire length of its surface of contact with power. On the contrary, sex is the most speculative, most ideal, and most internal element in a deployment of sexuality organized by power in its grip on bodies and their materiality, their forces, energies, sensations, and pleasures. (1980a, 155)

Foucault's reconception of power as a capillary and ubiquitous force, a force whose flows, intensities and resistances animate the social body and all knowledge formations, concedes no outside to this process. According to Foucault, society is organized in terms of 'discursive practices', ways of knowing which include language and representation as well as modes of behaviour, perception and deportment such as dress, regimes of cleanliness and self-care, the architectural organization of bodies, systems of belief and so on. Foucault originally drew a distinction between the discursive and the non-discursive but came to the conclusion in his later work that the division was untenable.[5] However, in this seemingly minor corrective Foucault underlined the social or cultural nature of nature, for with no outside sociality/the discursive, even the body's 'raw' perceptions of pain, pleasure and desire become expressions of subtle, social forces rather than absolute, or fixed, biological truths.

In her discussion of Foucault's work on *Herculine Barbin* (1980c), Butler explains the implications of Foucault's insistence that knowledge is coextensive with power. Foucault offers Herculine's journals, together with the medical records that document h/er ambiguous anatomy, as an insight into the disciplinary 'care' through which an apparently anomalous body is made legible and, one might assume, docile. We will not be surprised to learn that what have since become routine medical practices in the sexual normalization (re/assignment) of newly born babies had clumsy beginnings with the birth of modernity in the nineteenth century. However, Butler is keen to make a more contentious point about the constitutive aspects of power and its many guises. Foucault's most valuable contribution to the reconceptualization of power was to acknowledge its perverse productivity and ubiquity. Thus, power for Foucault is not merely a negative, juridical energy that represses, prohibits and prevents. If all knowledge, including self-knowledge, is an articulation of power, then it would be misguided to think, as we might in the case of Herculine Barbin, that s/he possessed an essential identity that pre-existed the prying medical and juridical intrusions of the state. Admittedly, domestic practices such as mothering, modes of dress, hygiene rituals and forms of play would already have inscribed Herculine's body with a specific sense of itself. Yet these 'private' practices are not outside the historical specificity of sociality's requirements: in other words, they are not epiphenomenal to what comes to matter as the body's underlying truth.

Although Foucault's work, in the main, represents an assault on emancipatory politics and the easy appeal to a 'before power', the difficulty in relinquishing such modes of thinking is underlined in Foucault's own tendency to romanticize the past as a time of untrammelled 'bucolic' and 'innocent' pleasures, a time of heterogeneous possibility prior to the univocity of the law. Butler is certainly critical of this nostalgia. And yet this recourse to an emancipatory politics reappears in Butler's work as well, as we saw in the case of the melancholic homosexual whose true desire/identity is forbidden by the incest taboo. If power is constitutive and ubiquitous such that even the resistance *to* power is actually the (re)articulation *of* power, then the conventional identity of 'power' is significantly reconfigured. For what can it be measured against? And how do we think about justice, agency and responsibility if individuals and their behaviours are animated by forces which they haven't authored? Unfortunately, Butler's appreciation of the law's perversity interprets its errant productivity as an alibi for hidden forms of repression. This reversion to a juridical notion of power whose intricacies, when all is said and done, are reducible to control is certainly curious, because Butler is obviously wanting to conjure something else. And yet her concluding summation to this section illustrates an inability to do so:

> In effect, s/he [Herculine] embodies the law, not as an entitled subject, but as an enacted testimony to the law's uncanny capacity to produce *only* those rebellions that it can guarantee will – out of fidelity – defeat themselves and those subjects who, utterly subjected, have no choice but to reiterate the law of their genesis. (1990b, 106; emphasis added)

If we are persuaded by Butler's overall argument, namely, that power is perverse, we must query a teleological interpretation of power that ascribes it with goal-oriented intentions. Such an approach anthropomorphizes 'the subject power' as if it possesses the univocity and intention of the humanist subject. Instead of psychologizing power, Foucault's work suggests that power evokes, and is, a force-field of logics/behaviours/social demands whose different intensities will cross each other (out) in ways that cannot be subsumed within structuralism's repressive conformities. Foucault underlined the generative or productive nature of power when he described it as perverse. However, Butler ignores this more transgressive reading by eliding perversity with a sort of *calculated* negativity, as if power is compelled to toy with us, to seduce us into different ways of being and thinking that will inevitably be thwarted. Here, we see that Butler's notion of power assumes not just anthropological pretension, but inasmuch as power and knowledge are coextensive for Foucault, Butler rolls this into a sort of teleological omniscience with theological resonance. One is reminded of Gloucester's fatalism in *King Lear*: 'As flies to wanton boys, are we to the gods;/They kill us for their sport.'

Once again we witness how the vigour of Butler's argument can be strangely undone by this recuperation of the very commitments her work contests elsewhere. Why, for example, does Butler open the field of political analysis with critical energy and promise only to inadvertently close it down in her conclusions? We are left to wonder if Butler's reading can be sustained more forcefully, or if perhaps there is something in the way she explicates her commitments that defeats her stated purpose. The emerging contradictions in Butler's argument deserve careful consideration: suffice it at this juncture to at least note their emergence and to flag them for later discussion.

To return to the final section of *Gender Trouble*, in an extended discussion of Wittig's work which dilates on the earlier analysis we see some of the main ingredients in Butler's notion of 'performativity' take recognizable shape. We will recall Wittig's refusal of the nature/culture distinction, and her argument, glossed here by Butler, that 'there is no distinction between sex and gender; the category of "sex" is itself a *gendered* category, fully politically invested, naturalized but not natural ...' Wittig goes on to explain that '[b]ecause "sex" is a political and cultural interpretation of the body, there is no sex/gender distinction along conventional lines; gender is built into sex, and sex proves to have been gender from the start' (Wittig, in Butler 1990b, 112–13). Butler supports Wittig's conviction here, as well as her general explanation of how the body's most intuitive perceptions of itself are produced and internalized as original. Language manufactures the 'reality effect' of sexual discriminations according to Wittig, by naming and imbuing body parts with particular (heterosexist) functions. Language 'casts sheaves of reality upon the social body ... stamping it and violently shaping it' (Wittig, in Butler 1990b, 115). Indeed, the reiterative practice of locutionary acts produces material meanings and effects which assume the status of the commonplace, 'the way it is'.

Butler certainly dismisses Wittig's suggestion that a subject could pre-exist, or escape, cultural representations and practices. However, she judges Wittig's understanding of the material efficacy and disruptive possibilities of language an important contribution to this field of inquiry. 'Wittig refuses the distinction between an "abstract" concept and a "material" reality, arguing that concepts are formed and circulated within the materiality of language and that that language works in a *material* way to construct the social world" (1990b, 119). Butler also acknowledges the powerful effects of Wittig's fiction and the fragmentations and transvaluations that her language achieves, 'enact[ing] an alternative disfiguring and refiguring of bodies' (1990b, 125). The transformative provocations in Wittig's writing, coupled with Butler's conviction that our lives assume their significance through the structural play of language, provoke her to insist that it is *within* language, not outside it, that the possibility of different sensual lives can be discovered.

The conclusion to *Gender Trouble* challenges foundational assumptions about the natural body and its sexual morphology and sexuality. Butler's aim, to consider how corporeality might be *materially* reconceived and therefore lived, must refuse any appeal to an 'outside of discourse', a 'before culture', which could operate as a natural alibi for a set of political preconceptions. Drawing on Foucault's conviction that the body is a surface of cultural and historical inscriptions which together produce its apparent facticity, Butler will also contest appeals to the body's interiority, its secret depths or hidden truths. For Butler, sexism and heterosexism operate as regulatory norms to organize the pluralities of bodies/desires into fictional coherence, a coherence which then assumes factual status. However, unlike Wittig, Butler's political intervention does not aim to replace one set of factual claims with a more accurate set of counter-claims, but rather to explore how the body's 'truth' is a reflexive performance wherein the body rewrites itself though 'acts, gestures, enactments' (1990b, 136).

In the practices of 'drag, cross-dressing, and the sexual stylization of butch/femme identities', Butler discovers an interesting disruption of the conventional discrimination between 'imitation' and 'original': '[i]n imitating gender, drag implicitly reveals the imitative structure of gender itself – as well as its contingency' (1990b, 137). What makes such parodic performances work is not their simple change of place, where the act underlines and preserves an original mismatch of bodies and behaviours. Gender is inherently parodic because without a substantial reference point to provide explanatory stability gender becomes a 'corporeal style' whose discontinuous reiterations dramatize its contingency. Clearly, Butler is contesting any appeal to a fixed foundation here, arguing instead that although gender attributes *appear* to express or reveal a prior sexual identity, the performance of gender actually installs that origin as its natural justification.

In the conclusion to *Gender Trouble* Butler anticipates her critics by acknowledging that she has significantly dismantled the conventional logic that authorizes political activism and even rejected the notion of emancipation. If the politics of identity cannot be secured in shared experience and if the subject is not a viable agent who can author a different destiny, then envisaging an alternative future seems impossible. However, Butler's 'performative politics' is not a simple rejection of such 'reference points' but a more nuanced attention to their complexity, for the notions of agency and identity do not dissolve when they are regarded as the embedded effects of cultural forces:

> . . . to understand identity as a *practice*, and as a signifying practice, is to understand culturally intelligible subjects as the resulting effect of a rule-bound discourse that inserts itself in the pervasive and mundane signifying acts of linguistic life. Abstractly considered, language refers to an open system of signs by which intelligibility is insistently created and contested. (1990b, 145)

Although Butler's 'performative politics' must wrestle with/in the rule-governed operations of language:

> [t]he subject is not *determined* by the rules through which it is generated because signification is *not a founding act, but rather a regulated process of repetition* that both conceals itself and enforces its rules precisely through the production of substantializing effects . . . all signification takes place within the orbit of the compulsion to repeat. (1990b, 145)

Accordingly, agency emerges in the interstices of those different and often competing rules and the variation of their repetition. Indeed, it is in the slippage, dissonance, or even contradiction of their repetition that the subversion of identity becomes possible, if not inevitable. Butler conceives these rules in juridical terms, as 'an injunction' to *be* a given identity: 'a good mother . . . a heterosexually desirable object, . . . a fit worker' (1990b, 145). However, it is in the friction and unavoidable incompatibility of these demands that failures to conform must occur, and subversive or non-normative subjectivities must arise. Thus, Butler's insistence that the subject doesn't pre-exist these cultural regimes of identity formation is not meant to deny the subject's existence as the embodied expression of these converging and competing demands. Butler's understanding of the subject, identity and agency is therefore an implicated one which locates the possiblity of contestation and change in the very structures through which subject formation and its corollaries are generated. 'For an identity to be an effect means that it is neither fatally determined nor fully artificial and arbitrary' (1990b, 147).

Yet, there is a problem here, for although Butler's project is to rethink the terms of 'the political' in more mired yet pragmatically plausible ways, an insistent algorithm appears throughout her work whose logic compromises its provocation. This is not to detract from her considerable achievement but to take her argument seriously and engage with its detail. To this end, a more sustained analysis of her understanding of 'language', arguably the key to her entire oeuvre, will be explored in the next section. At this juncture, however, and as part of the summation of *Gender Trouble*'s accomplishment, the more problematic aspects of the argument will simply be noted.

It is perhaps ironic that Butler's stated intention to reconfigure power as a productive, generative and perverse force is hobbled by an enduring and overriding commitment to power's juridical identity and repressive 'psychology'. For example, power is envisaged as a 'naturalizing' (dissembling) force whose primary 'purpose' is restrictive and normalizing. Although Butler finds enormous value in Foucault's way of perceiving power's productivity, her conceptual commitment to Lacanian psychoanalysis, a theory dependent on the notion of prohibition, leads her to blur, or even ignore, these theories' incompatibilities. Foucault's contribution to the theorization of power represented a critical intervention against psychoanalysis, structuralism and the 'repressive hypothesis' which such thinking presumed. Given this, Butler's attempt to marry these approaches without specifically addressing their disjunction produces peculiar tensions and contradictions in her argument which are managed by the book's structural organization.

Butler consistently represents power, *first and foremost*, in terms of prohibition, injunction and repression. But do we need to personify and imbue power with such attributes? In other words, must power be possessed of an intention, a goal or desire at all, let alone *one* that is inherently normative and negative? Butler's own argument, at least in certain places, would certainly contest this, and yet she consistently attributes power with design – 'the injunction to reconsolidate naturalized identities' (1990b, 146). Only if we presume that power's intention is to realize a constrained and repressive outcome does it make sense to then say that power 'fails' to 'compe[l] bodies to approximate' its dictates. For without a specific goal or purpose it isn't at all clear that 'bodies are compelled to approximate' anything. What *are* power's 'dictates' if power is the dispersal of energies whose constitutive differential animates the entire social field and *all* its expressions?

The most troubling concern that emerges in this concluding section then, and it mirrors an organizational fault line that runs through *Gender Trouble*, is whether a Foucauldian understanding of power *can* be made compatible with a psychoanalytic one. Butler's 'performative politics' assumes that the law must continually repeat itself in order to reinstantiate itself as a fixed, foundational truth: the will to repeat is a will to stabilize identity. However, this interpretation, namely that the law 'intends' to oppress and prescribe by denying its mutation, seems spurious. Surely the incoherence of the law, its *inherent* instability, is publicly evident in the very process of its interpretive performance. To take a juridical example, the law is an argument not simply about the contingencies of a particular case, but concomitant to this, about the *acknowledged* ambiguities in the letter of the law itself. As any televiewing audience knows only too well, the law is pliable, sometimes unpredictable, and its advocates actively work with this. From this perspective, there is no need to interpret the law's mutation as a failure to hold true. Why does Butler *need* to assume that the law's purpose, power's purpose, is to deny or repress the vagary of its identity?

Chapter 3

Gender, Sexuality, Performance – Bodies that Matter: On the Discursive Limits of "Sex"

Biology. Anatomy. Substance. *Physis*. Nature. These words signify the gravity of being, the weight of the world and the shared corporeal dimension of human life. They indicate limits, restrictions, foundations – the touchstones of existential and political opportunity. As we saw in the previous chapter, the substantive self-evidence of these determinations is hotly contested, and *Bodies that Matter* weighs into the argument by insisting that cultural processes generate natural foundations. Butler justifies this reversal of order by marrying several linguistic approaches, and her methodology will be closely examined in the next few chapters. What follows here is a more general discussion of what Butler means by the dynamic complexity and political vitality of 'materialization', and why these complex processes are severed from something unknown and unrepresentable; something 'other' that we would normally understand as the physical substance and self-evidence of matter. For it is clear from the subtitle of *Bodies that Matter* – namely, *On the Discursive Limits of "Sex"* – that Butler's argument is intentionally circumscribed and does not extend to an enduring, ahistorical referent, or 'thing itself'. Instead, her analytical attention is captured by the dynamic psychosocial interactions that explain the mutability of bodies – their evolving pleasures, desires and self-definitions. Although physical reality and its representation are certainly entangled for Butler, her intervention explains this intricacy in terms of their actual difference:

Just as no prior materiality is accessible without the means of discourse, so no discourse can ever capture that prior materiality; to claim that the body is an elusive referent is not the same as claiming that it is only and always constructed. In some ways, it is precisely to claim that there is a limit to constructedness, a place, as it were, where construction necessarily meets its limit. (1998a, 278)

... the linguistic effect is not the same as the referent that it fails to capture. This is what allows for a variety of ways of making reference to something, none of which can claim to be that to which reference is made. (1998a, 279)

Butler aims to disrupt those styles of reasoning that justify their conservative intentions by referring to an 'original cause', a manoeuvre meant to neutralize and conceal a moral and political prejudice by making it seem inevitable and even necessary. This is plainly illustrated in the dictum 'biology is destiny'. However, it would be absurd to insist that biological and anatomical considerations have no relevance to questions of subject formation and human being generally: the contention arises when we consider *how* we perceive the actual meat of the body's biological interiority and anatomical reality. Butler will argue that what appears in all its obviousness as the materiality of brute existence, the 'before culture', is just that, an *appearance* which is ciphered, transformed and phantasmatically invested by social regimes of significance. Consequently, 'life itself', if we can risk such an expression, will always exceed the models, metaphors and representations that attempt to access and understand it. Indeed, it is this discrepancy, this incommensurability between physical reality and attempts to make sense of it, that grounds a critical practice. In sum then, Butler will argue that the nature of nature is given identity and meaning through cultural processes and, perhaps more importantly, that the difference between the original material (Nature) and its later 'materialization' (Culture) will actually incite the reinvention of bodies and pleasures.

If anatomy is not an original, accessible referent that can explain or determine what we mean by sex, gender and sexuality, then every category that presumes this direct correspondence becomes something of a question mark. As we saw earlier, Wittig argues that the conventional categories of sexual identity are made to answer the normalizing regimes of heterosexuality. But if anatomy is *entirely* bracketed out, then the potential instability of these identities becomes even more apparent. Why, for example, do we attribute *the* female body with the stability of a fixed referent, as if it is 'something shared' that can secure femaleness and explain lesbian sexuality? In an examination of similar questions, Jonathan Dollimore offers further grist for the identity mill with the 'endearing instance' of Sukie de la Croix. Sukie is a gay man who finds himself attracted to Troy, a straight African-American woman. Happily, after days of worrying that Troy's charms have compelled his own sexual identity to 'do a turnabout', a friend reveals that Troy is a very convincing transvestite. But is the anxiety that Sukie feels about his true identity and desire actually resolved by this information? Dollimore thinks not, asking us to consider if:

> ... we [can] confidently say "who" or what Sukie "really" desired in this scenario *prior to* the point of his friend's disclosure about Troy ... Was this desire really heterosexual, or was it bisexual? Is it not just possible that he was being other than consciously disturbed by his own homosexuality? And even assuming we could decide, what difference does his friend's disclosure actually make? In short, gay identity, as distinct from homoerotic fantasies of identification, far from being the direct social counterpart of our desires, may in part be a protection against them – including those desires sanctioned by the identity. (1996, 525)

Dollimore remains unconvinced that Troy's penis has really settled the question of identity for either Troy or Sukie, and in 'The Lesbian Phallus and the Morphological Imaginary' (1993a) Butler investigates why such 'mistakes' are not only possible, but also inevitable. Her meditation on the puzzle of anatomy opens with a detailed reference to Freud's essay, 'On Narcissism: An Introduction' (1991a), where the analyst dilates on the nature of the libido. According to Freud, the libido has a fluid and quantitative dimension, and it is through the accrual and diminution of its 'love energy' that the personal significance of bodily experience is registered, or felt. The movement of these excitations is likened to an economy because its forces are cathected, or invested, through fluctuating intensities across the body, as well as outwardly, into the bodies of others. Evidence of this fluctuation can be seen in the response to pain and injury. When the amount of libidinal energy available to the subject proves insufficient, energy must be 'called in' and reinvested. As it is withdrawn from external love objects and transferred into the self, the subject can become entirely self-absorbed by the experience, even amplifying the pain and eroticizing its intensity in the process. The reverse is also true: when the subject's attentions are distracted from the pain, the perception of injury can diminish significantly, or even vanish. Freud provides a perfect illustration of pain's subjective registration in the time-less example of a nagging tooth. Here, the compass of throbbing agony extends well beyond its physical origin to envelop the subject's entire being: 'concentrated is his soul ... in his molar's [jaw-tooth's] aching hole' (Freud, cited in Butler 1993a, 58).

When we think of pain we think of the body's unmediated and most urgent reality, and yet the experience of pain shows radical variation across different cultural and social contexts, as well as marked shifts within the individual subject.[1] The example of toothache suggests that pain is physically *and* psychically induced, and registered accordingly. And yet the need to use a conjunction in this simple description of hybrid causes tends to install biology as the first, or original cause, whose effects may be modulated by cultural and subjective influence. However, the logic of this temporal two-step that separates nature from culture is increasingly confused as Freud extrapolates from the experience of toothache to other examples of libidinal self-investment, including hypochondria. In the latter instance of imaginary physical ailments, the explanatory direction from biological causes to their subjective interpretation is reversed: here, pain arises from psychical forces that manifest as biological symptoms. Noting the 'theoretical indissolubility of physical and imaginary injury' in Freud's argument, Butler makes two interesting observations:

> This position has consequences for determining what constitutes a body part at all, and, as we shall see, what constitutes an erotogenic

body part in particular. In the essay on narcissism, hypochondria lavishes libido on a body part, but in a significant sense, that body part does not exist for consciousness prior to that investiture; indeed, that body part is delineated and becomes knowable for Freud only on the condition of that investiture. (1993a, 58)

Anticipating Lacan's argument in 'The Mirror Stage' (1977a), Freud believed that a sense of self was acquired through the realization of body boundaries as the child underwent a developmental separation from the (m)other. As we see in the following comment, there is a clear suggestion that the body can only be apprehended *as* morphology: '[t]he ego is first and foremost a bodily ego; it is not merely a surface entity, but is itself the projection of a surface' (Freud, cited in Butler 1993a, 59). And yet the suggestion that self-discovery is provoked by the conscious experience of physical excitation or pain presents us with something of a quandary. How can consciousness be a derivative of corporeal self-discovery if it is already present at its initiation? Butler notes that 'it is fundamentally unclear, even undecidable, whether this is a consciousness that imputes pain to the object, thereby delineating it – as is the case in hypochondria – or whether it is a pain caused by organic disease which is retrospectively registered by an attending consciousness' (1993a, 59). In this account, self-perception is not attributed to biological causes alone (assuming there could be such a thing), but to an erotogenicity that renders the *idea* of a particular body part coincident with the phenomenology of its perception.

Underlining the sexual nature of libidinal self-attention, Freud suggests that 'the familiar prototype [*Vorbild*] of an organ sensitive to pain, in some way changed and yet not diseased in the ordinary sense, is that of the genital organ in a state of excitation' (Freud, cited in Butler 1993a, 59). Butler remarks on the attribution of masculinity in Freud's use of the definite article, *the* genital organ, yet any sexual specificity vanishes when we realize that other erogenous zones can substitute for the genitals and respond similarly. The redistribution of libidinal investment from one body part to another means that while the genitals are prototypical of this variable process, they do not inaugurate this chain of substitutions. As Freud explains, '[w]e can decide to regard erotogenicity as a general characteristic of all organs and may then speak of an increase or decrease of it in a particular part of the body' (Freud, cited in Butler 1993a, 61).

The ambiguity in Freud's clarification provides Butler with a degree of critical purchase, because if male genitals retain no ontological privilege or priority in fact or symbolic value, then there is more going on than the simple displacement of an original phallic (masculine) privilege and the transference of its erotogenicity to other body parts. Indeed, what can it mean to talk of '*its* erotogenicity', as if the phallus is one single organ, a penis? As Butler describes it, '[t]o be a property of all organs is to be a property necessary to *no* organ, a property defined by its very *plasticity, transferability*, and *expropriability*' (1993a, 61). And if the properties and capacities of a body part are truly contingent, acquiring recognition *as a result* of libidinal investiture, then 'the phallus' is a term for the *process* of investiture – for the action of delineating, identifying and eroticizing. It follows from this that the identity and integrity of any one organ will always be compromised because its 'singling out' is a relational discrimination whose construal involves, and retains, its context. Butler's explanation of what is going on in that 'jaw-tooth's aching hole' provides a helpful illustration of this congested and condensed network of referral, 'a punctured instrument of penetration, an inverted vagina dentata, anus, mouth, orifice in general, the spectre of the penetrating instrument penetrated'. Even the tooth's identity is ambivalent, as 'that which bites, cuts, breaks through, and enters' and yet 'that which is itself already entered, broken into' (1993a, 61).

But why should libidinal transfer be described in terms of paternity? Through a sliding metonymy of references that presumes the identities it is trying to explain, Freud conflates the generative power of the phallus with the male organ. As we have seen, the phallus is more accurately understood as a productive *process* of delineation through which entities/body parts emerge into identifiable significance. When this transformative dynamism is arrested and likened to a thing-like property however, man appears to *have* the phallus, just as woman appears to *be* this erotic and valued object; a commodity possessed or exchanged between men. This sexualized matrix of oppositional functions and subject positions organizes other divisions, whereby woman becomes a being of passivity to man's activity, a vacuous instrument for his agency and pleasure, a vulnerable body that requires protection from his invulnerable one, a dumb body that depends on the superiority of his more evolved reasoning capacities. Because the phallus (woman) is figured as an attachment, a tool to be used and manipulated, this heterosexual economy of signification understands man as an *in*corporeal being: he may *have* a body and certainly desires *it*, yet he is not, himself, body. Despite its cartoon logic, these 'natural' associations exert an insidious gravitational pull on the way we conceptualize sexual identity as well as what constitutes a legitimate mode of attachment and exchange/sexual intercourse.

With such considerations in mind, we can appreciate why Butler's reflections on the lesbian phallus are provocative. Is it really a failed copy of a male original, a substitute for woman's bodily lack and its corollary – the sexual incapacity of the lesbian? As Butler comments: 'Of interest here is not whether the phallus persists in lesbian sexuality as a structuring principle, but *how* it persists, how it is constructed, and what happens to the "privileged" status of that signifier within this form of constructed exchange' (1993a, 85).

Freud's own conviction about the nature of libidinal energy thwarts an explanatory return to a single origin because the libido is a *field* of energy whose uneven distribution throughout the body motors the infant's self-discovery. Of course, the notion of 'self' in this description is somewhat premature because the infant's self-recognition as a bounded individual among many has yet to take place: prior to this, the plenum of the world is *self-same* with the child. And here we need another qualification and one we will have good reason to return to, for the infant's apparent coincidence with the world need not imply a homogenized unity, or undifferentiated plenitude *before* the cut of difference (culture/language/individuation). It is important to appreciate that this originary 'self-same' is a congested and entangled scene of non-coincidence and referral. In other words, the differentiation that the infant perceives remains overwhelming because its complexity

has yet to be 'properly' interpreted and apportioned a meaningful place. Because the infant is inherently fragmented at first,
and therefore fractured and certainly 'multiple' in what might be
described as its primordial identifications, attachments and
desirings (because the other is (also) itself), Freud described
human sexuality as constitutionally *bisexual* and *polymorphously
perverse*. Although Freud doesn't provide an exact explanation of
bisexuality and questioned its meaning and implications
throughout his life, it is clear that the difference between
masculine and feminine, or male and female, is so muddled by
the notion that the binary coordinates of sexual difference can't
explain the term.[2] For this reason, rather than think of
bisexuality in ways that already presume identity (e.g. male plus
female), it might be more useful to consider bisexuality as the
splitting of desire that renders all identity incoherent and
perverse from the start: deprived of a single origin, a unified
identity, intention or goal, the teleological notion of sexuality that
segregates bodies and pleasures into distinct identities and
appropriate practices has no natural foundation.

It follows from this that the attribution of the libido's origin to
the male organ and the inevitable valorization of the penis as *the*
generative site (the phallus) is an imaginary illusion that can only
be sustained if the transgenesis of libidinal energy is denied and
repressed. And yet, although this denial naturalizes privilege the
very nature of its deceptive manufacture will remain a structural
flaw in its maintenance – something Butler considers 'the
promising spectre of its destabilization' (1993a, 63). The system's
fragility is again underlined when Freud describes erotogenic
discovery and self-preoccupation in terms of illness, pain and
suffering. As we saw earlier in the example of hypochondria, a
case of narcissistic self-absorption, the subject's fascination is
expressed by delineating a particular body part as inherently
fragile, sick and in need. By making the theatrical performance of
illness exemplary in the eroticization of the body – 'a libidinal
projection of the body-surface which in turn establishes its
epistemological accessibility' (1993a, 63) – Freud underlined the
social fabrication of sexuality and its potential concatenation with
illness. In *The Ego and the Id* (1991b) Freud draws an even closer

link between sexuality and illness when he finds that the
hypochondriac's self-preoccupation is, as Butler describes it,
'symptomatic of the structuring presence of a moralistic framework of guilt' (1993a, 63). According to Freud, guilt arises
because the internal dynamic of narcissistic self-possession must
be externalized towards objects and other subjects if we are to
experience a normal sexuality. To refuse this social demand by
reinvesting in the self is to take a guilty pleasure, and yet this
pleasure is fraught with ambivalence: on the one hand, its
unsanctioned satisfaction exacts physical illness and suffering, but
on the other, if the resulting illness effectively deceives society
then the underlying narcissism is affirmed. Can the difference
between pleasure and pain be decided in this example?

Aware of the ambiguous possibilities that attend an 'eroticized
hypochondria', Butler notes that if conformity to regulatory
sexual ideals requires prohibition and the threat of pain, then the
failure of these interdictions, or their qualified success, must
induce irregular outcomes. '[T]hey may delineate body surfaces
that do not signify conventional heterosexual polarities. These
variable body surfaces or bodily egos may thus become sites of
transfer for properties that no longer belong properly to any
anatomy' (1993a, 64).

The possibility of the lesbian phallus makes its appearance at
this juncture. However, before returning to this provocative
proposition we should underline that the link that connects
sickness with narcissism, the love of self, is something Freud
associates with homosexuality, the love of self-same. What is
purported to be an inwardly directed, primitive and pre-social
libidinal energy must be turned around in a heterosexual
economy and aimed towards others. Freud argued that the
successful taking on of these heteronormative requirements
coincides with the development of a conscience – the will to
conform to social regulation. Thus, if the propriety of sexual
identity depends on 'the introjection of the homosexual cathexis'
(1993a, 65), then the effective maintenance of normality is built
on the pain and guilt that now attaches to this unsanctioned and
prohibited pleasure. As Butler describes this tortured outcome,
'[t]his prohibition against homosexuality *is* homosexual desire

turned back upon itself; the self-beratement of conscience *is* the reflexive re-routing of homosexual desire' (1993a, 65).

However, Butler suggests that the pain of self-beratement and denial does more than simply abandon a love object, for something 'productive' is also at work as the psyche organizes the body into an imaginary schema of meaningful parts. If the body *appears* in the form that it does because it is a living history of felt significance, then the social prohibition against certain love objects will re-form those libidinal investments to preserve and memorialize them:

> If, then, as Freud contends, pain has a delineating effect, i.e., may be one way in which we come to have an idea of our body at all, it may also be that gender-instituting prohibitions work through suffusing the body with a pain that culminates in the projection of a surface, that is, a sexed morphology which is at once a compensatory fantasy and a fetishistic mask. And if one must either love or fall ill, then perhaps the sexuality that appears as illness is the insidious effect of such a censoring love. Can the very production of the *morphe* be read as an allegory of prohibited love, the *incorporation* of loss? (1993a, 65)

Butler's argument moves from Freud's meditation on narcissism to Jacques Lacan's reformulation of Freud's theory in 'The Mirror Stage' (1977a) and 'The Signification of the Phallus' (1977b). Lacan will argue that the child's apperception of itself as a coherent and bounded entity in space means that it must learn to identify itself from another's perspective, that is, from an external vantage point that it cannot occupy. Using the child's recognition of itself in a mirror as an analogy for this more general process of speculation, Lacan attributes the resulting morphology, or bodily outline that the child assumes, to a dynamic vacillation between projection and misrecognition. Several things are important here. First, the disjunction between the infant's perception of its amorphous ubiquity, an 'all over the place' that Lacan punningly describes as an 'hommelette', and the specular idealization of itself as a coherent (other) entity with control and agency, will never be resolved. This means that the ego is, and will remain, a *bodily* ego, whose identity is not so much a fixed property as an ongoing dynamic of *re*-cognition and mutation. Second, Lacan will also argue that the morphological schema that inaugurates the ego is also the threshold of the visible world. In other words, how we perceive the difference between people, objects and their inter-relationships (the shape and definition of otherness) will be extruded through a corporeal imaginary which has constitutive force: the subject *is* this process, where the differentiation of world and ego emerge in the same reflex/reflection. As Butler summarizes:

> As imaginary, the ego as object is neither interior nor exterior to the subject, but the permanently unstable site where that spatialized distinction is perpetually negotiated; it is this ambiguity that marks the ego as *imago*, that is, as an identificatory relation. Hence, identifications are never simply or definitively *made or achieved*; they are insistently constituted, contested and negotiated. (1993a, 76)

Butler certainly agrees with Lacan that the child's bodily ego is 'peopled' with others, inasmuch as its very anatomy is in-formed with social relations and their dynamic conversions. Indeed, the possibility of a lesbian phallus will depend on the psychosocial open-endedness of the body's perceived anatomy. However, Butler finds something disturbing in the way Lacan's argument seems to have it both ways. He explains the organizational logic of the Symbolic order, those cultural and linguistic structures into which the child is interpellated, as a *given* system of binary identifications whose positions are determined by a transcendental signifier – the phallus. And yet he also insists (and we are reminded here of Lévi-Strauss and the more general claims of structuralism) that the Symbolic order exceeds *specific* cultural or social ascriptions for it is the universal principle of differentiation that motors all languages. For this reason, Lacan will echo Freud by insisting that the phallus should not be confused with the penis, or indeed with any organ or particular imaginary effect. But what can be done if we accept this thesis? As Butler's critical energies are focused on the need to contest political inequities, her concern is that Lacan's 'explanation' has the performative consequence of investing the penis (and masculinity) with the symbolic privilege accorded the phallus, and in a way that places the male organ's political significance *beyond question.*

Through a close reading of the twists and turns in Lacan's argument, Butler uses the analyst's own explanation to question the distinction he makes between the Symbolic order and the Imaginary, that wishful process of representational identification that enables the infant to overcome (and deny) its inadequacies:

> If the position for the phallus erected by Lacan symptomatizes the speculative and idealizing mirroring of a decentered body in pieces before the mirror, then we can read here the phantasmatic rewriting of an organ or body part, the penis, as the phallus, a move effected by a transvaluative denial of its substitutability, dependency, diminutive size, limited control, partiality. The phallus would then emerge as a symptom, and its authority could be established only through a metaleptic reversal of cause and effect. Rather than the postulated origin of signification or the signifiable, the phallus would be the effect of a signifying chain summarily suppressed. (1993a, 81)

Butler's questions remind us that for *any* body part to be delineated as identifiable and separate, the body's overall erotogenicity and signifiability will be involved; indeed, the body part will emerge from a process that incorporates the whole of the body in the 'part's' transvaluation. Lacan would surely agree in principle that the phallus can take myriad imaginary forms other than the penis, including objects. However, when Butler takes Lacan at his word and raises the gender-troubling spectre of a lesbian phallus, the political investments which align phallic mastery with 'the mutually exclusive trajectories of castration anxiety and penis envy' (1993a, 84–5) are no longer straightforward. Without recourse to a stable point of origin that can anchor the vagaries of the bodily ego as well as its dispositions of desire, all identity, including sexual identity, is rendered ambiguous. Lacan's work would certainly concede this point, or even underline it. However, Butler perceives something more subversive in the 'contradictory formulation' of a lesbian phallus that 'crosses the orders of *having* and *being*':

> [I]f men are said to "have" the phallus symbolically, their anatomy
> is also a site marked by having lost it; the anatomical part is never
> commensurable with the phallus itself. In this sense, men might be
> understood to be both castrated (already) and driven by penis envy
> (more properly understood as phallus envy). Conversely, in so far
> as women might be said to "have" the phallus and fear its loss (and
> there is no reason why that could not be true in both lesbian and
> heterosexual exchange, raising the question of an implicit hetero-
> sexuality in the former, and homosexuality in the latter), they may
> be driven by castration anxiety. (1993a, 85)

If the bodily ego *necessarily* incorporates such phantasmatic
cross-overs, then normative bifurcations of sexual identity and
desire must involve a failure of fit which is borne, or made legible,
by 'marginal' subjectivities, even though it pertains to everyone.
Importantly, Butler rejects the idea that the so-called margin is
constitutively different from the centre, an insight that complicates a pluralist politics of inclusion as well as its inverse – the
privileging of the margin as a site of play and possibility outside
the repressive structures of heteronormative identity. Instead,
what is emphasized in Butler's argument is that structures of
subject formation have no central point of authorization, no
overarching logic of non-contradiction that separates heteronormative forms of exchange from those that seem so different. If
structures of identification are so thoroughly messy, implicated
and ambiguous for all of us that the difference between who has
the phallus and who is the phallus is a social and political
determination that can't be anatomically decided, then the
seeming invariance of phallic reference is a performative fiction.

As we have seen, Butler focuses on the Lacanian thesis that the
phallus inaugurates the signifying chain and sets it into motion
because it is radically incommensurate with its representational
substitutions. Lacan's thesis is certainly a provocative proposition
because the givenness of an origin and an entity are replaced by
process and irresolution – a dynamism in which the lived
significance of anatomy is in play and the invariance of reference
is undone. This is the leverage point where Butler locates her
question about the conflation of the penis with the privileged
signifier of the phallus; if 'the phallus symbolizes only through

taking anatomy as its occasion, then the more various and unanticipated the anatomical (and non-anatomical) occasions for its symbolization, the more unstable that signifier becomes' (1993a, 90). Consequently, if the lesbian can have and be the phallus at the same time (as Lacan's separation of the phallus from the penis must imply), then the facticity of the body and related notions about what a body can and can't do are subjected to 'an aggressive reterritorialization' (1993a, 86). In other words, and ironically, the implications of a lesbian phallus acknowledge the complex dimensions and sensate reality of *everyone's* phantasmatic anatomy as well as the myriad objects and expressions that desire can assume.

In a way, it could be argued that Butler's argument fleshes out the more radical aspects of Freud's notion of polymorphous perversity and originary bisexuality. However, just as the psychoanalyst was unable to maintain the radical implications of this fundamental perversity against the political backdrop of Victorian life, and Lacan, in turn, found the penis and phallus magnetically connected, it seems fair to ask if Butler's feminist intervention is, in the end, similarly compromised.

What has been established is that Butler's work rests on a vigilant interrogation of the coherence and purity of identity, especially the presumption that identity is there from the start. And an important platform in her critical strategy has been to return to anatomy in order to reconceive its referential stability. In sum then, Butler has argued that an individual's body boundary (the imago, or phantasmatic body) is an erotic surface whose individual perception is forged from social relations that are always evolving and shifting the body's contours and desires. Importantly, the delineation of this imaginary anatomy is borne from the pain of loss, and it remains a fragile and unstable 'edifice' for just this reason. Forged from failure and incapacity, it is unable to re-present an ideal it cannot have and cannot be: it is a misrecognition of itself, a 'dissimulated effect', 'a fetishistic mask', 'a compensatory fantasy' of grieving melancholia for what is now prohibited (1993a, 65).

Consistent with this rather forlorn scene of unrequited desire that motors production, we will recall that Butler seizes on the erotics of hypochondria, the ability of pain to rewrite loss as pleasure, to exemplify this general process of transvaluation: it delineates body parts, ailments and objects as erotic memorials to a maternal loss that exceeds representation. The ability of the body to *be* something other than it seems, to incorporate the alien as itself, explains why Butler describes masculine, heterosexual melancholy as a '. . . refusal to grieve the masculine as a possibility of love; [just as] a feminine gender is formed (taken on, assumed) through the incorporative fantasy by which the feminine is excluded as a possible object of love, an exclusion never grieved, but "preserved" through the heightening of feminine identification itself' (1993a, 235). The uncanny manifestations of prohibition are further underlined in the comment, '[i]n this sense, the "truest" lesbian melancholic is the strictly straight woman, and the "truest" gay male melancholic is the strictly straight man' (1993a, 235).

It is politically significant to appreciate, as we do in these transfigurative examples, that prohibition is never purely negative. But here is the rub. Although things are certainly not as they seem in this account, Butler's critique of identity remains tethered to its unproblematic status as foundation. Instead of the bisexual perversion that renders sexual identity improper and undecidable from the start, *and* forever after, Butler's analysis effectively untangles the ambiguity to reveal a truth behind the counterfeit. If we are to understand female identity and femininity as essential attributes that define the mother, then the masquerade of identity-forming reversals that her (supposed) loss engenders makes sense. But surely this is far from the case. The mother is deemed a phallic mother because s/he lacks nothing. S/he is the (w)hole, the world, the parenting plenitude of transfiguration which, at one and the same time, expresses the child's 'own' difference from itself; the constitutive difference that drives the child's desire for itself/another. In this scene of morphogenesis where identity is never established once and for all, the m/other is a ubiquitous figure. And if s/he is never simply lost or absent, then what is the status of the term 'misrecognition' that founds Lacan's thesis as well as the masquerading ruse in Butler's description of the 'truest lesbian' and the 'truest straight man'?

Do we gain a better sense of the complex operations of identity formation if we consider that this involved complicity is not reducible to duplicity? This is a difficult and elusive point that requires careful exegesis. For example, we will recall that Freud interprets the hypochondriac's sickness as a foil for narcissistic self-attention, a foil whose pleasurable suffering incorporates the guilt that attends the production of a body that will not conform to the demands society makes of it. The narrative resolution of what to do with this initial pre-possession that is defined *against* society is to hide 'it'. But why should we assume that the plenitude of primordial erotogenicity (pre-possession) is an individuated 'something' that is radically separate from an outside when child and world, or what we retrospectively bifurcate into these identifying differences (internal and external, self and other), are originally consubstantial?[3] 'Consubstantial' in this sense evokes the 'sameness' of an identity that endures (invariance) through morphogenesis (variation). This is the real puzzle, a veritable brain twister, and its dimensions defy the sort of explanatory 'resolution' in Butler's reversal. The very notions of 'sameness' and 'difference', 'homo' and 'hetero', are not just *implicated* – a notion that presumes their segregation before it is compromised. If identity is *never* given, and these terms of reference can never be segregated, then the constitutive paradox of identity becomes strange indeed.

But why is so much at stake in the subtleties of this entanglement? Butler's own argument helps us here, for she repeatedly questions the commonality that subtends the description of the *homo*sexual, and even judges the existence of a lesbian sexuality 'an impossible monolith' (1993a, 85). The developmental narrative that discovers a primordial, narcissistic self-possession at the origin, and *naturally* equates this with the love of self-same (homoeroticism), will quite logically presume that social maturity and the acquisition of a conscience are more evolved achievements – the proper attributes of the heterosexual who is male. Butler is certainly aware of the danger in this logic, as we see in this 'cautionary note':

The pathologization of erotogenic parts in Freud calls to be read as a discourse produced in guilt, and although the imaginary and projective possibilities of hypochondria are useful, they call to be dissociated from the metaphorics of illness that pervade the description of sexuality. This is especially urgent now that the pathologization of sexuality generally, and the specific description of homosexuality as the paradigm for the pathological as such, are symptomatic of homophobic discourse on AIDS. (1993a, 64)

Quite clearly, the violence of homophobia can't be attenuated by such moral appeals if the logic that discriminates homosexual from heterosexual identity remains intact. Homophobia, misogyny and racism are nourished by the notion that a primitive hypersexualized self-absorption precedes the social, and this original incapacity is defined against social legitimacy. To argue that 'legitimacy' is questionable because it represses and maintains something it claims to abhor certainly addresses the problem, yet it remains committed to the narrative's political order – from primitive to civilized, from same to different, from the maternal order to the paternal symbolic. To posit the social as a second-order frame of reference, a regulating force that befalls the infant (who initially lacks it) and leaves it at a loss, understands identity as 'something' that is either present *or* absent, true *or* fictional. To congeal the process of differentiation into a circumscribable commodity or system, secured against an outside, is the same as reifying the phallus, the process of identify*ing*, into a thing – the penis. Can the ingenious provocation that Butler offers us in 'the lesbian phallus' keep this question of origins moving, and in a way that might resist a return to identity's foundational truth?

Chapter 4

Language, Power, Performativity –
Bodies that Matter: On the
Discursive Limits of "Sex"

Judith Butler's ability to engage so many different issues is enabled by her appreciation that apparently unrelated intellectual endeavours may be bound and committed to the same logic and conceptual foundations. In the following discussion we will explore one of the most important examples of this foundational excavation in Butler's work, namely, her investigation of the ontology of language/discourse and related debates about cultural constructionist arguments.

In *Bodies that Matter: On the Discursive Limits of "Sex"* (1993a) we are given her most detailed explanation of why the language question carries such political importance. Butler begins her introduction to a corporeal politics by foregrounding the contamination that surrounds and inevitably undermines the integrity of a pure referent, arguing that there can be no access to materiality outside or before signification and, by extension, no access to a pure materiality of bodily life that is separate from language.

Nevertheless, we retain a sense that there must be some sort of marginal overlap between ideality and matter because Butler denies that 'the body is simply linguistic stuff' while at the same time insisting that '[the body] bears on language all the time' (1993a, 68). The problem arises when we think of this natural foundation as something that precedes, and therefore exceeds, language and thought, because if this is truly the case then our ability to comprehend it will prove futile. In response to this dilemma, Butler strives to infuse matter with a constitutive energy and efficacy that will disrupt the impasse in this deeply divided logic, for if matter can be rescued from its location as both prior and passive in regard to cultural meaning-making, then conventional understandings of corporeality and matter shift considerably. Accordingly, the need to reconfigure materiality becomes the pivot of Butler's argument with the discourse of construction, a need made evident in the following passage:

> In an effort to displace the terms of this debate, I want to ask how and why "materiality" has become a sign of irreducibility, that is, how is it that the materiality of sex is understood as that which only bears cultural constructions and, therefore, cannot be a construction? ... Is materiality a site or surface that is excluded from the process of construction, as that through which and on which construction works? Is this perhaps an enabling or constitutive exclusion, one without which construction cannot operate? What occupies this site of unconstructed materiality? And what kinds of constructions are foreclosed through the figuring of this site as outside or beneath construction itself? (1993a, 28)

The difficulty in Butler's project is considerable for she has to juggle a critique of the discourse of construction while still defending its most basic tenets. Wanting to secure a hearing from those whose patience with such arguments has been exhausted she begins by offering some basic reassurances about her own approach. As the discourse of construction is routinely perceived as linguistic idealism, Butler willingly acknowledges the insistent reality of bodies. She grants what she calls 'the alleged facts of birth, aging, illness and death', and agrees that some minimal existence must be allowed 'sexually differentiated parts, activities, capacities, hormonal and chromosomal differences' and so on (1993a, 10). The complication, however, is that to concede the existence of certain bodily facts is also to concede a certain interpretation of those facts. Butler conveys the conundrum by asking, '[i]s the discourse in and through which that concession occurs ... not itself formative of the very phenomenon that it concedes?' (1993a, 10).

There is an unavoidable convolution in Butler's position

because it targets two quite different expressions of the same argument, an argument that uncritically chooses sides in the materiality/ideality split. To explain this, if we situate this debate within feminism then those who claim to represent real women without recourse to inverted commas will assume they have access to the truth of (the) matter, as if the compelling facts of women's lives are self-evident. According to this view, signifying practices are the mere vehicles of such truths, having no formative input of their own: although they may well be regarded as inadequate it is assumed that any deficiency can be corrected. The other side of this debate stresses the constitutive force of signifying practices, concluding that we have no access to an extra-linguistic reality because the truth of its apparent facticity is produced in language. Butler is in obvious sympathy with this latter position but disagrees with the conclusion that often accompanies it. Although she agrees that we cannot access an 'outside language' that is unmediated by language, she does not take this to mean that we can, or should, try to censor any mention of this outside. Indeed her thesis tries to emphasize that the received grammar of the debate will necessarily produce an exteriority, an outside discourse that is nevertheless internal to discourse. Given this, the task is not to deny or presume to exclude this materiality but to analyse the '*process of materialization that stabilizes over time to produce the effect of boundary, fixity, and surface we call matter*' (1993a, 9).

Butler's analysis of corporeality focuses on the repudiation of matter as 'other', because its rejection is a key ingredient in subject formation. When difference from a valued norm is made synonymous with deficiency, any deviation can be pathologized as a flaw or fault. More importantly, the implicated history that links the denigration of matter with 'natural deficiency' is difficult to acknowledge because the mark of deficiency that unfairly attaches to certain bodies seems 'naturally' to explain their abject status. Within the terms of this tautology, the inherent failure of these abject bodies to 'make proper sense' renders them unintelligible, beyond representation and therefore outside the concerns of the democratic process. Refused entry into the domain of the fully human, these outcasts are then aligned with the unruly dangers of the natural, the brutish and the animal, in other words, with the threat that is perceived to emanate from matter itself. Butler's goal is to disrupt the economy of this logic by asking, '[w]hat challenge does that excluded and abjected realm produce to a symbolic hegemony that might force a radical rearticulation of what qualifies as bodies that matter . . .?' (1993a, 16).

The 'outside of language'

Butler's discussion of the discourse of construction acknowledges the necessity of speaking in terms of an 'outside' or 'beneath', a 'before' or 'beyond' language and discourse. Indeed, this is not something that can be avoided. But if the difference between ideality and matter is a discursive distinction, then the political associations that attach to their differences *can* be accessed and contested. Butler's point is that if language and discourse constitute the meaningful dimension of lived reality, and there are many meanings, then the enclosure of language is not a prison-house: on the contrary, language and representation are fluid structures whose internal complexities allow different outcomes and possibilities.

In sum then, Butler's desire to engage the structured move-ment of differentiation *within* language does not preclude the existence of an outside language that truly does exceed our perceptions and representations; it's just that the human condition bars access to it. Accordingly, the perception and representation of this outside, despite its convincing transparency and our sense of its immediate accessibility, will always be a language effect – a cultural production. Butler's reliance on the overarching term 'culture' as the explanatory category that *contains* this shifting process surely makes the point. In other words, language and culture are mutually implicated – indeed, some would say they are one and the same.

And yet, by privileging the term 'culture' in this way, the identity and sexualized hierarchy between matter and ideality, nature and culture, and body and mind, are surreptitiously reinstalled. Although Butler's strategy might be described as placing the first term in these pairings into question, thereby rendering it unknown, the inevitable effect is to actually expand the second term by evacuating, or entirely erasing, the first. Butler's intervention is obviously meant to reinterpret both terms, and she achieves this when she shows that what we thought was Nature is really 'nature', that is, Culture. However, we need to appreciate here that Butler has actually drawn a line of clarification between a realm of knowledge and political contestation, namely Culture, and what pre-exists it – Nature (now more accurately represented as 'under erasure', or crossed out – ~~Nature~~). Thus, Butler's critique of the inseparability and contamination of nature and culture *as concepts* is founded upon an absolute separation between ~~matter/Nature~~ and culture/ ideality. According to Butler then, we can avoid the confusion between matter and its representation if we remember that '[t]o return to matter requires that we return to matter as a *sign* . . .' (1993a, 49).

As the title *Bodies that Matter* makes clear, Butler's aim is to contest and expand 'the very meaning of what counts as a valued and valuable body in the world' (1993a, 22). The argument that the body's substance is a sign rather than a fixed solidity or prescriptive referent is furthered in the happy coincidence between the words 'matter' and 'materialize'. While these words evoke a *notion* of physical substance, these signs are also synonyms for 'meaning' and the larger semantic process of meaning-making:

> To speak within these classical contexts of *bodies that matter* is not an idle pun, for to be material means to materialize, where the principle of that materialization is precisely what "matters" about that body, its very intelligibility. In this sense, to know the significance of something is to know how and why it matters, where "to matter" means at once "to materialize" and "to mean." (1993a, 32)

Butler's reworking of the terms through which corporeality is conventionally comprehended certainly challenges their received meanings. However, it should now be apparent that the in-itself of matter, the substantive something that Butler's minimal, if qualified, concession to hormonal and chromosomal differences acknowledges, is not at all the object of her analysis. Ironically perhaps, its absence is required in order for her thesis to have some purchase. Our sense of the materiality of matter, its palpability and physical insistence, is rendered unspeakable and unthinkable in Butler's account, for the only thing that can be known about it is that it exceeds representation. Beyond cultural intelligibility, the existence of this external stuff ensures that our understanding of an outside, inasmuch as it is discourse dependent, can only be the dissimulation of an outside that *appears* as matter.

At this point it might prove helpful to follow Butler's engagement with the political theorist and cultural analyst Slavoj Žižek because her assessment of his work's usefulness involves a more general conceptualization of what language is and how it works. In the chapter 'Arguing with the Real', Butler explores the uses and limits of psychoanalysis in Žižek's work with the aim of developing a more inclusive 'theory of political performatives and democratic contestation' (1993a, 20). Butler challenges the reasoning that exiles certain subjects outside the pale of humanity proper, as though they do not matter, by interrogating the way in which limits are determined and meanings ascribed. Taking the structure of the sign as an exemplary indication of how such limits and exclusions are produced, Butler will argue that the limit falls short of itself, that is, it ultimately fails to secure its integrity or identity. As Butler argues that our world is a world of representation/language, her argument concentrates on the way that language 'materializes' its own limit and exteriority. According to Butler, a true separation from this 'constitutive outside' cannot be achieved because 'identity always requires precisely that which it cannot abide' (1993a, 188). Thus, the question behind Butler's close analysis of the very machinery of language is, '[h]ow might those ostensibly constitutive exclusions be rendered less permanent, more dynamic?' (1993a, 189).

In Žižek's use of psychoanalysis, a theory that locates subject formation within the internal structures of language, Butler perceives a foundational commitment to a notion of the limit as prohibition and injunction. Although she agrees with Žižek that the subject does emerge through a set of repudiations and foreclosures, she disputes the need to mark foreclosure in absolute terms, as the Real. For if the Real is truly outside symbolization as Žižek, following Lacan, suggests then we are left with the following dilemma. 'Consider the rhetorical difficulty of circumscribing within symbolic discourse the limits of what is and is not symbolizable' (1993a, 190). The Lacanian notion of the Real is the lack of lack, a sort of plenitude that pre-exists the definitive cuts and divisions, the discriminations and valuations, of language and culture. Interestingly, the originary integrity or self-sufficiency of the Real will be appropriated by the Symbolic order (The Law of the Father) through a sort of flip-flop of its potentiality. And this results in the cultural domain of language and representation assuming a sort of fullness and sufficiency, whereas the corporeal or natural ground of existence that seems to precede language reverts to a primal deficiency; a lack or loss deemed feminine in its very essence. The effect of equating difference with lack means that an original plenitude seems to be severed from the social, or Symbolic order, and this way of conceiving difference rehearses the threat of castration and loss, as well as the gender identifications and associations that go with it. Given the labour of feminist critics over the years to explain and disrupt the inherent phallocentrism of Lacan's schema, it is not surprising that Butler is critical of Žižek's approving adoption of it. Butler explains the insidious implications in Žižek's commitment:

> Žižek argues that "the Real is [language's] inherent limit, the unfathomable fold which prevents it from achieving its identity with itself. Therein consists the fundamental paradox of the relation between the Symbolic and the Real: the bar which separates them is *strictly internal to the Symbolic*." In the explication of this "bar," he continues, "this is what Lacan means when he says that 'Woman doesn't exist': Woman qua object is nothing but the materialization of a certain bar in the symbolic universe ..." (1993a, 279)

This conflation of woman with what is barred from existence, that is, with what falls short of full inclusion into the Symbolic order, equates woman with the black hole of the unrepresentable;

the ineffable space of the Real. As the political agenda endorsed by this reading is disastrous, Butler argues that the limit of the Real cannot be exempted from interrogation and placed outside discourse. In the presumptive givenness of the Real's purported ahistorical endurance, a symbolic normativity of sexed subjectivity and sexuality is sanctioned:

> That there are always constitutive exclusions that condition the possibility of provisionally fixing a name does not entail a necessary collapse of that constitutive outside with a notion of a lost referent, that "bar" which is the law of castration, emblematized by the woman who does not exist. Such a view not only reifies women as the lost referent, that which cannot exist; and feminism, as the vain effort to resist that particular proclamation of the law ... To call into question women as the privileged figure for "the lost referent," however, is precisely to recast that description as a possible signification, and to open the term as a site for a more expansive rearticulation. (1993a, 218)

Butler must rupture the bar that cuts presence from absence (lack, the Real), and language from what is considered prior to, or not language, in order to open the possibility of a revaluation of conceptual economies and subject positions. In other words, she must engage the mode of production of these determinations, the hidden indebtedness to 'the feminine' whose disavowal equates femaleness with bankruptcy. She explores the metaphysics of presence that oppose identity to difference as presence to absence (I am what I am by dint of not being that) with the aim of refiguring difference as a shared, generative force within whose transformational energies the sense of a fixed identity (as presence to self) is radically destabilized.

In order to achieve this, and despite her criticisms of the way that Žižek makes use of psychoanalysis, Butler finds his discussion of 'political signifiers' particularly useful for this project. Žižek argues that political signifiers such as 'woman' should not be regarded as descriptive designations of actual subject positions because they do not represent pre-given constituencies. Žižek's qualification is an important one because:

No signifier can be radically representative, for every signifier is the site of a perpetual *méconnaisance*; it produces the expectation of a unity, a full and final recognition that can never be achieved. Paradoxically, the failure of such signifiers ... fully to describe the constituency they name is precisely what constitutes these signifiers as sites of phantasmatic investment and discursive rearticulation. It is what opens the signifier to new meanings and new possibilities for political resignification. It is this open-ended and performative function of the signifier that seems to me to be crucial to a radical democratic notion of futurity. (Butler 1993a, 191)

Butler is taken by the suggestion that political signifiers can be sites of mobilization and contestation, identificatory anchors whose constitutive force is transformational. Via Žižek then, she is able to rupture the fixed identity of the signifier and to insist that it is constantly mutating and therefore constitutionally incapable of erecting a secure barrier against its 'own' exteriority. If women and other socially abjected subjects are themselves subjected to/through these same significatory transformations then their existence and its significance must be determined *within* the Symbolic order. Unfortunately, Žižek's reading of the bar as an absolute prohibition, as if the cut of castration is a definitive fact, reaffirms an 'outside discourse' in derelict terms of trauma and castration. Thus, by appropriating Lacan's notion of the Real to explain this foreclosure, Žižek actually endorses the inevitability, the indisputable necessity, of this violent inheritance of abject subject formation. In view of this, Butler's intervention is important because it illustrates that the bar is not an absolute, fixed barrier, but a process of demarcation, an ongoing *attempt* to bar or draw a line that is never finished. The installation of the bar as an absolute frame achieves *the effect* of both discovering and repudiating that outside as inherently deficient and *naturally* base.

By interrogating the foundation, or what is supposedly 'given' as the indifferent ground of valuation, and by discovering that it is forged from the same political determinations as other significatory practices, Butler is able to dispense with the foreclosure of the Real entirely. This strategy is surely reasonable enough when considered against Žižek's equation of difference with absence/nothing. However, inasmuch as Butler's theoretical approach continues to rely upon a notion of absence in other places in her argument, it is not surprising that the political problems that plague Žižek's position make an uncanny reappearance in Butler's. This is evident in Butler's elaboration of how the significatory energy of transformation and desire is received by 'empty signs which come to bear phantasmatic investments of various kinds' (1993a, 191). But how is anything straightforwardly 'empty', given Butler's own refutation of nothingness? We are left to wonder how this significatory support in the body of the sign can bear phantasmatic projections that form the constantly changing ground of meaning and legibility. For it seems that the sign's 'workability' is compromised by an internal emptiness that nevertheless possesses the functional capacity to receive and resignify. What can it mean to project phantasmatic projections onto emptiness, as if the body of the sign is nothing, and bears nothing? If these projections are also significations, as Butler suggests, then why is the differential of giving and receiving understood through presence and absence, value and lack, male and female, mind and body, that mirrors a phallocentric logic? And how is the difference of phantasmatic projections translated into anything given their apparent lack of identity, their non-existence?

Butler's commitment to the sign

Although the above point might seem relatively unimportant in terms of Butler's general achievement and the broader concerns she addresses, her investment in a very conventional notion of the sign's identity and its internal components informs her overall understanding of what language is and how it works. Butler's explicit attempt to avoid Žižek's conflation of woman with absence founders on this enduring commitment, and this in turn compels her to read difference against identity, presence against absence, and to reiterate the conservative implications of this signifying economy. In this context, it is important to appreciate that the Saussurean sign has had many interpreters, and even Ferdinand de Saussure himself was somewhat confounded by the sign's complexity. Despite this, it is the Lacanian interpretation of the sign that holds sway in much cultural criticism, and Lacan's presumption that a bar of prohibition separates the Real from the Imaginary and Symbolic (Culture) is repeated in a different form when he separates signifier from signified. Instead of puzzling over the nature of these differences, Lacan simply assumes them, as does Butler, and in a way that places Nature, now under erasure, entirely outside this 'system'.[1] Put simply, the bar marks off the cultural order (glossed as 'language') as an identifiable and delimitable object of study. Admittedly, the bar of difference cannot be overcome or put aside. If this could be achieved it would reinforce the notion of difference as something superfluous; an extraneous supplement whose absence would not be missed. Rather, the problem with the Lacanian understanding of the sign is that the identity of the bar itself is completely barred from scrutiny – and this is a similar point to the one Butler makes when she questions the way Žižek exempts the Real from analysis. Unified, undifferentiated and therefore utterly impermeable, the bar represents pure prohibition. Castration is absolute. Thus the bar or limit becomes a guarantee of property that encloses the concept sign within the domain of language/culture, and segregates subjects and their attributes accordingly. By extension, it also contains the intent of the sign, however wayward, within the domain of signification or meaning.

Butler's faith in the conceptual topography of the sign and its expression through presence and absence must inevitably hit up against a difference deemed to be *absolutely exterior* to culture/language, even though it is produced within it. In sum then, Butler's interrogation of the bar and its abjecting results relocates the cut of prohibition rather than calling foreclosure and absence itself into question. In the assumption that the integrity of the bar is itself barred from analytical scrutiny, the bar's identity is reified as pure negativity. The bar of prohibition *internal* to the sign is therefore banished only to re-emerge as the sign's defining *outer limit*, the separating barrier between language and what is not language, now Culture and ~~Nature~~. The bar now surrounds the sign and protects its internal content, the domain of culture (language), from the threat of ~~Nature~~ unveiled. But something shifts here. It is important to appreciate that the bar that is internal to the sign represents the threat of castration, that is, the threat to the wholeness and autonomy of *man's* identity. However, the exterior limit of the sign in its more comprehensive identity as the language system (culture) represents the threat to the identity of *humanity* itself once its abjected exiles have been properly recognized as meaningfully human. On the other side of this line of defence lies an unspeakable threat – the body of ~~Nature~~, the substance of radical alterity.

If we use this interpretation of the bar, or prohibition, as a clue to how we conceive of the law, we can see that by unifying the law in this way we render resistance as a reactive and fairly futile response to the instrumental force of a negating and absolute power. As we saw in a previous chapter, Butler makes this very same point in her criticism of the Lacanian, or perhaps more accurately here, the Kristevan scheme that separates the Imaginary from the Symbolic registers. As she queries:

> ... does this view of resistance fail to consider the status of the symbolic as immutable law? And would the mutation of that law call into question not only the compulsory heterosexuality attributed to the symbolic, but also the stability and discreteness of the distinction between symbolic and imaginary registers within the Lacanian scheme? It seems crucial to question whether resistance to an immutable law is *sufficient* as a political contestation of compulsory heterosexuality, where this restriction is safely restricted to the imaginary and thereby restrained from entering into the structure of the symbolic itself ... feminine resistance is [thereby] both valorized in its specificity and reassuringly disempowered ... By accepting the radical divide between symbolic and imaginary, the terms of feminist resistance reconstitute sexually differentiated and hierarchized "separate spheres." ... resistance ... cannot enter into the dynamic by which the symbolic reiterates its power and thereby alter the structural sexism and homophobia of its sexual demands. (1993a, 106)

By contesting the nature of the division between the domain of language as the law of the Symbolic, and the domain of the Imaginary as the pre- or proto-linguistic, Butler successfully undermines several assumptions, namely, the straightforward identity and integrity of the Symbolic order; the integrity/

identity of the self-present male subject; and the marginalization and even erasure of women and other denigrated subjects in this system of identity formation. And yet, Butler conceives the power of the law as the power to name, to assign and to delimit, so that the very act of naming is considered a violence of sorts. It follows from this that the law itself appears as a unified force, just as the name appears coherent. Yet this notion of murderous destruction ignores an interesting ambiguity at the heart of the word 'violence', for the force of rupturing and breaching confounds destruction with/in creation.

By reading power's purpose in terms of an ultimate negation, prevention, constraint or prohibition, Butler is unable to consider the possibility, indeed the inevitability, wherein a political rearticulation is already at work *within* the law, and can arise from *within* the name itself. By foreclosing this sense that the law is inherently perverse (and that the signifier is already a scene of disarticulated potential), Butler is forced to locate hope for change in the signifer's historicity, that is, in the anticipation that it may suffer some distortion over time, (only) when it is repeated. Butler dilates on this point by noting that hegemonic norms require maintenance: the law must be laid down again and again. And this constant re-invocation of the law is likened to a form of speech act, suggesting that '[d]iscursive performativity appears to produce that which it names, to enact its own referent, to name and to do, to name and to make' (1993a, 107). Butler takes the apparent closure in this tautological reflex as proof that the legitimacy of discursive authority is a fiction. It cannot ground itself in an original authority because the act of citation, the repetitive difference that is language, is a practice of perpetual deferral to a source now lost or absent: '... it is precisely through the infinite deferral of authority to an irrecoverable past that authority itself is constituted. That deferral is the repeated act by which legitimation occurs. The pointing to a ground which is never recovered becomes authority's groundless ground' (1993a, 108).

Acknowledging Jacques Derrida's complication of the notion of repetition, however, Butler explains that a deconstructive *iterability* disrupts the sense of repetition that assumes a series of separate moments in time, and she goes on to explain why a Foucauldian understanding of discourse and power will not sit comfortably with Derridean *iterability*. As Butler herself has noted, a deconstructive reading would suggest that repetition, 'the always/already', inheres even within an apparently isolated act or event. And further to this, Derridean 'textuality' cannot be subsumed to the Foucauldian understanding of 'the discursive', with its presumptions about social regulation and social possibilities. What emerges from a Derridean reading then is that there is never a simple failure, or absence, of production, and any and every 'act' is, in a sense, efficacious in myriad ways, many of which will not be apparent. But where does this leave Butler's position, given its requirement of an original, referential failure?

Although this may seem like a finicky point the implications are considerable. Butler's reading assumes that there once was a definitive origin/referent, a discrete entity quite separate from its re-presentation in language/discourse. It follows from this that language, inasmuch as it is perceived as a second-order *construct* or *substitute* for something now lost, founds its very identity on a notion of difference as separation. In other words, Butler's argument must assume that a now inaccessible reality precedes its re-presentation, a re-presentation whose status is that of fantasy and fiction, the phantasmatic field of *cultural* interpolation. Butler's insistence that these fictions remain powerful because they 'real-ize' effects reverses the logic of causality but does not contest causality's discrete, linear discriminations, nor 'the how' of causality. But it is this linear sense of temporality and its corollary concepts of causality (efficacy, origin and end) that become muddled within the space/time complexity of Derridean *iterability*. As Butler herself concedes, if a 'moment' emerges *within* differentiation then it can have no simple exteriority.

The political implications of founding an explanatory model on absence

The relevance of this for re-reading power becomes clearer if we return to Žižek's notion of 'political signifiers'. Žižek argued that signification should not be given the status of description for there is a permanent recalcitrance, or failure of fit, between the referent and symbolization. This gap, which implicitly identifies and contains difference, explains why Žižek might determine that the descriptive fact of the referent is more accurately understood as a phantasmatic construct, the desired product of hegemonic structures that are open to contestation. Endorsing this view, Butler emphasizes that political possibility is actually generated from the discrepancy between language and the actuality of the referent. As she explains here with specific reference to the signifier 'woman', '[t]hat the category ["women"] can never be descriptive is the very condition of its political efficacy' (1993a, 221).

Butler eschews description because it is a gloss for what is purportedly timeless, essential and outside the performative iteration, or alteration, of language. However, this founding exemption ties Butler once again to a notion of difference as substitution, wherein difference is read as the sign of something else, of some originary loss or absence. Loss and absence are therefore essential to Butler's reading for she locates the problematic nature of identity in the constitutive *failure* to recuperate this loss. Because of the inevitable *incompleteness* of identity in this assumption, both Butler and Žižek understand any appeal to integrity in terms of *phantasmatic illusion*. However, against this psychoanalytic reading the emergence and transformation of identity within Derridean iterability is not explained by an originary absence whose result is an inevitable impairment.

Butler is fully aware of the unfortunate consequences of an oedipal logic that aligns and fixes sexual positionalities. As her discussion of Žižek's argument reveals, if the pre-discursive is read through the logic of lack, then a sexualized and racialized battery of incontestable prescriptions seems to be endorsed by nature itself. Indeed, Butler is adamant on this point, and her argument is most persuasive when she maintains its importance. For example, in her discussion of Chantal Mouffe and Ernesto Laclau's theorization of radical democracy and its relevance to Žižek's thesis, Butler makes another assault on the insidious equation of difference with lack by questioning the compatibility between the Derridean logic of the supplement and the Lacanian notion of lack that these theorists assume. To explain this, Mouffe and Laclau find the promise of an open-ended political futurity in the constitutive antagonisms and contingencies of identity formation. Making a similar point to Žižek's, they explain the possibility of renegotiating identity in terms of an inevitable failure of ideological structures to fix themselves as fact. Butler interprets Laclau to locate these contingencies and antagonisms within social relations that he ambiguously describes as being '"outside" of posited identity' (1993a, 194). Given this, Butler's question concerns the status of Laclau's statements about 'the antagonizing force [that] *denies* my identity in the strictest sense' (1993a, 194):

> The question, then, is whether the contingency or negativity enacted by such antagonizing forces is part of social relations or whether it belongs to the real, the foreclosure of which constitutes the very possibility of the social and the symbolic. In the above, it seems, Laclau links the notions of antagonism and contingency to that *within* the social field which exceeds any positive or objectivist determination or prediction, a supplement within the social but "outside" of posited identity. (1993a, 194)

As we have seen, Butler criticizes Žižek for locating this constitutive antagonism and contingency outside the social as such, in the Lacanian Real, and we can see why she might prefer Laclau's account. However, as Laclau also explains the production of identifications in terms of 'lack' while at the same time drawing on the Derridean notion of supplementarity, Butler inquires, '[i]f the "outside" is, as Laclau insists, linked to the Derridean logic of the supplement (Laclau, NRRT, 84 n. 5), then it is unclear what moves must be taken to make it compatible with the Lacanian notion of the "lack" ...' (1993a, 194). Butler's quandary is explained by her reading of the Derridean supplement as an *internalized* exteriority, one whose convoluted 'attachments' return it to the realm of social reinscription.

Yet despite Butler's move here, and it is an important one, her own commitment to a notion of lack or absence means that her question concerns the appropriateness of its location – either inside or outside the social. We should realize that the negative in its pure form assumes a radical break, a gap, a nothingness; a clear separation between one thing and another that prevents connection and turns questions about indebted inter-productivities into a nonsense. And yet the identity of lack *as such* is not in question here. Consequently, the puzzle over the compatibility of the Derridean notion of supplementarity with the Lacanian notion of lack is significantly restricted by the erroneous assumption that Derridean supplementarity never really leaves the social world. Although Derridean supplementarity is indeed about an internalized exteriority, Butler assumes that the identity of that interiority is 'given.' Because Butler believes that language begins and ends with human culture, her intervention is meant to underline this fact: reinscription and political possibility must be confined to the social arena. After all, surely ~~Nature~~ is *prescriptive*.

The complexity of identity formation that Butler concedes to a word, to an individual, or to a particular social milieu, is not granted to 'entities' such as 'language', 'the social', or 'the cultural'. Although forces rupture and differentiate the respective interiorities of these identities, it seems that their identifying borders remain immune to this same disturbance. Butler conceptualizes the limit of these entities as separate supplements, supplements which are not themselves open to the logic of supplementarity. However, by foreclosing the domain of differentiation, productivity and mutability in this way, Butler builds her critique of difference (as lack) upon the very logic that she contests; the logic that equates difference with absence. Put simply, the substance of ~~Nature~~ and whatever else culture exteriorizes as properly outside itself, is rendered *utterly* absent and therefore insignificant by being placed under erasure.

A Derridean intervention into the conflation of language with culture

But what difference might the Derridean logic of the supplement make to this way of thinking, given that Butler herself strives to accommodate its puzzle? Is it inevitable that *différance* returns to lack, if not immediately, then in the final instance, as Butler assumes? There would be few scholars familiar with contemporary theoretical work on language who would be surprised to hear that Derridean *iterability* or, here, *supplementarity* refigures temporality and spatiality such that our understanding of terms such as 'description', 'essence', 'origin' and 'ground' are radically altered: all of these terms assume a defined spatial and/or temporal locatability and fixity that Derrida's work unhinges and disperses. Given the assault of deconstruction upon foundational notions such as these, it isn't much of a stretch to include 'the body' and 'matter' within the orbit of these interrogations. Yet does this assault reiterate Butler's position, or could it return us to questions about corporeal substance that, although in a very different way, actually further the stated aims of Butler's work?

As we have seen, Butler deploys the term 'matter' rather than 'substance' because the former is a synonym for significance/ signification. To think of substance is to think of the very meat of carnality that is born and buried, the stuff of decay that seems indifferent to semiosis. Substance evokes the soil of groundedness itself – the concrete, tangible, and essential thing-ness of things. To avoid using the word 'substance' is surely a careful decision on the part of a writer whose stated interest is the materiality of bodies. What risk, then, is Butler's sustained avoidance of this term trying to minimize?

The concept 'substance' has a long history of philosophical engagement that certainly complicates commonsense assumptions that perceive the body's interior densities as self-evidently (made of) 'substance'. Butler ignores this vulgar, lived sense of bodily life, focusing instead on the body's surface as the site of engagement. She does this because she regards the body as a shifting text, or discursive effect, whose perceived outline is constantly changing. These transformations of the body's morphology are regarded as a form of reckoning that 'contours the bodily matter of sex' and 'set[s] the limits to bodily intelligibility' (1993a, 17). Butler draws on the work of several theorists in order to elaborate this notion of a contour/threshold, and renders it in terms of interpellation (Althusser), enunciation

(Benveniste), body imago (Lacan) and inscription (Foucault). Through these different approaches she invests the surface/ threshold with activity, and elaborates how contour-*ing* is a process of ongoing signification, contestation and reinscription. As conventionally understood, signification is a play of form, and substance is excluded from this activity. By remaining on the body's surface its internal meat needn't be mentioned: it is simply excluded from corporeal reinscription, its process and registration. Thus, although signification is an operation whose very experience and possibility is registered and forged through the entirety of the body's biological and perceptual apparatus – our neurological maps, cognitive representations, sensate recordings, expressions and translations, and so on – Butler's thesis must refuse any suggestion that biological substance might be semiological in nature. Instead, and as we have seen, Butler draws a dividing line between ~~Nature~~ (the unknown, the 'before thought' and language) and Culture (the known, the thought, the articulated) on the surface of the skin. But how different is this assumption that the very stuff of knowledge is not *thoroughly* corporeal, from Cartesian dualism in its crudest form? What is it that actually creates and receives inscriptions if it is not the body's interior complexity? And if that interiority reads and writes those inscriptions (because it must be in the nature of biology to do this), then need we assume that flesh itself is outside, or before, textuality/language?

Butler is drawn to the Derridean notion of *différance* because it disrupts the logic of identity that figures difference as lack; in other words, if *différance* inheres *within* identity as the very force of its very possibility, then it can't be equated with deficiency, or the lack of identity: *différance* doesn't mark a need for restitution, propelled by a failure to be something, as the Lacanian model of difference assumes. Lacan argues that the break with the origin (the Other, Mother, ~~Nature~~) can never be repaired because the origin is irretrievably lost, inaccessible, gone: its misrecognition in substitute form is the only consolation. However, *différance* complicates this linear sense that time unfolds in a series of discrete 'moments' where the past is lost to the present. When

Derrida foregrounds implication, refusing to separate one thing from another, we are left with the unsettling and counter-intuitive suggestion that the origin continues to invent or be itself, albeit differently. Consequently, ~~Nature~~ (M/Other, the body, and all the feminized categories that mark difference as deficiency) is not re-presented by a substitute 'stand-in'. *Différance* mires the difference between substance and form, physis and ideality, nature and culture, in a way that can't be resolved, as Butler has done, by assuming that Culture's presence is secured by ~~Nature's~~ absence.

For Butler, the messiness of identification is only explicable because the substantive referent (intact in ~~Nature~~) is absent; hence, its textual replacement, woven from myriad cultural sources. But if the origin itself was always/already a congestion of emergent possibility from *within* whose differences Life evolves, where, then, is the radical break? If *différance* implicates all exteriority within interiority, then Culture is not a dissembling version of an entirely separate and primordial system.

Although Butler's intention is to animate matter and contest the conservatism of those who would return to an immutable ground, she doesn't consider the possibility that textuality, or *différance*, might *be* the ground. For if 'there is no outside of text', as Derrida suggests, then it is in 'the nature of Nature' to write, to read and to model.[2] If this sounds risky because it seems to return to biologism and its prescriptions, we need to remember that there is nothing immutable or *pre*scriptive about this ground. If the logic of morphing is the complex mutation and process of limit-ing, as Butler suggests, then this re-articulation is not restricted to semantics and the polysemous possibilities of linguistics.

The fiction of the self-conscious individual fully aware of his intentions and agent of his own destiny is quite clearly displaced here. However, if the humanist subject comes undone in the face of Nature's literacy, this unravelling does not stop with the critique of humanism. Butler constantly reminds us of the need for sustained contestation of the nature/culture division and why it matters, why this questioning is itself a political practice and why intellectual work at this interface will always be necessary. As she notes:

The relation between culture and nature presupposed by some models of gender "construction" implies a culture or an agency of the social which acts upon a nature, which is itself presupposed as a passive surface, outside the social and yet its necessary counterpart. One question that feminists have raised, then, is whether the discourse which figures the action of construction as a kind of imprinting or imposition is not tacitly masculinist, whereas the figure of the passive surface, awaiting that penetrating act whereby meaning is endowed, is not tacitly or – perhaps – quite obviously feminine. Is sex to gender as feminine is to masculine?

... This rethinking [of nature] also calls into question the model of construction whereby the social unilaterally acts on the natural and invests it with its parameters and its meanings. Indeed, as much as the radical distinction between sex and gender has been crucial to the de Beauvoirean version of feminism, it has come under criticism in more recent years for degrading the natural as that which is "before" intelligibility, in need of the mark, if not the mar, of the social to signify, to be known, to acquire value. (1993a, 4–5)

If we agree with Butler that there are unfortunate and enduring political implications in this last assumption and that we need to dispute its logic, then it is imperative that we question Butler's insistence, a form of reassurance, that 'to return to matter requires that we return to matter as a *sign*'.[3] The enclosure of the sign's identity, if accepted, will not provide a fertile and generative departure point for thinking the messiness of difference. Yet, by putting the sign into question and exploring and exploding its identity as Butler might encourage us to do in other contexts, matter appears *within* the horizon of our inquiry as a much more curious subject. And importantly, its appearance need not be veiled in substitute form as a cultural artefact.

Chapter 5

Language, Power, Performativity –
Excitable Speech: A Politics of the
Performative

Butler's analytical methodology is an active, evolving response to the queries and criticisms her arguments provoke. In *Gender Trouble*, she illustrates the fluid nature of identity formation through the trope of theatrical performance, the sense that identity is a staged artifice, a fantastic re-presentation with no natural stability. However, Butler came to question her use of drag to exemplify this process because it encouraged the misconception that mimicry and play are voluntary strategies: there was an implied sense that different subjectivities could be chosen, or tailored, to suit changing individual fancies. In *Bodies that Matter* Butler puts pay to this free-wheeling sense of performance, emphasizing that although agency and bodily materiality are discursive effects this doesn't make them easy to manipulate. Given this, Butler's specific interest is in how the social parameters of language and culture actually function to affirm certain subjects and to diminish and devalue others. How does a normative process of restraint and prohibition take effect and politically discriminate between identities? How are cultural evaluations imposed and naturalized as truths?

Butler's appreciation that language is a rather mysterious operation is of more than theoretical interest. Indeed, as we will see in *Excitable Speech*, Butler is eager to assess the analytical relevance of her argument by investigating several examples of hate speech which have come to prominence in US political life. Taking this opportunity to bring more rigour to her approach, she expresses some dissatisfaction with the theories of subject formation she had previously relied upon, especially what she calls the 'unilateral' and 'unnuanced' mechanism of discursive constitution offered by Michel Foucault (Butler and Bell 1999c, 164).

In *Excitable Speech: A Politics of the Performative* (1997b), this situation is repaired by a more detailed account of how the constitutive and materializing process of language actually works. After all, if the performative is the ' "linguistification" of the political field' (1997b, 74) as Butler suggests, then it seems reasonable to wonder how language can produce failure and conformity as well as unpredictability and innovation. What is it about language that allows such diverse outcomes to arise within one, enclosed system? More pragmatically, how can the very intelligibility of certain 'failed' identity formations be called into question if their lived reality is marked by abjection and placed outside the bounds of proper regard and comprehension?

In this revision of performativity Butler brings together several different theoretical approaches, all of them discussed in varying detail in previous writings; Louis Althusser's 'interpellation', J. L. Austin's 'Speech Act Theory', Jacques Derrida's 'citationality' or 'iterability' and Michel Foucault's 'discursive formation'. Importantly, Butler's perspective on language retains a felt, corporeal dimension, as we see in her focus on the wounding and hurtful power of words. And yet she will claim that although words can certainly injure, disable and render vulnerable, they can also validate, inspire and enliven. The puzzle that needs to be explored is poignantly captured in these opening remarks:

> When we claim to have been injured by language, what kind of claim do we make? We ascribe an agency to language, a power to injure, and position ourselves as the object of its injurious trajectory. We claim that language acts, and acts against us, and the claim we make is a further instance of language, one which seeks to arrest the force of the prior instance. Thus, we exercise the force of language even as we seek to counter its force, caught up in a bind that no act of censorship can undo. Could language injure us if we were not, in some sense, linguistic beings, beings who require language in order to be? (1997b, 1–2)

Language is not a mere instrument or tool in this account, a technology used to different effects by a sovereign subject who controls it. The complication here is that if we ourselves are an effect of language then the complexity of its ontology resonates with our own constitution. Consequently, our ability to command, censor and adjudicate language for our own purposes is radically compromised. But through what process are we incorporated into this social fabric? The relevance of this question is emphasized when we realize that for Butler the question of language is interchangeable with that of power.

In the work of the Marxist philosopher Louis Althusser, Butler is provided with 'a scene, as it were, with which to start to ask the question: what does it mean to appropriate the terms by which one is hailed or the discourse in which one is constituted?' (Butler and Bell 1999c, 164). Althusser offers a useful staging of the process yet one whose 'fabulous' example illustrates its paradox. Briefly, an individual is hailed or interpellated into society through an act of recognition and response to the call of another. In Althusser's concrete example it is a policeman who calls out 'Hey, you there!' (1971, 174), thereby dramatizing the call's implicit authority. As Althusser describes it, in the physical 'conversion' of turning around the individual becomes a subject, acknowledging that the call was *for* him, that '"it really is he" who is *meant* by the hailing' (1971, 175; emphasis added). The description implies that the individual is not alone and, indeed, Althusser notes that although there are others in the street, just one will turn back: '... (nine times out of ten it is the right one) ... believing/suspecting/knowing that it [the call] is for him' (1971, 174–5).

And so we are presented with a quandary. As Butler explains it, strictly speaking the one who answers the call cannot pre-exist the call if this moment of address initiates the subject's emergence. Yet in the very act of turning around the suggestion that we are witness to the inaugural trope of subject formation loses all credibility. We might wonder how one individual can self-select from the group of passers-by, understanding that a response implies responsibility, if s/he had not anticipated and, at least in some vicarious sense, already experienced the event.

Althusser surmises that perhaps this 'strange phenomenon ... cannot be explained solely by "guilt feelings"' (1971, 174), but whatever its cause it attests to an uncanny prescience. Butler describes the scene's significance without comment on its timing. 'The passerby turns precisely to acquire a certain identity, one purchased, as it were, with the price of guilt. The act of recognition becomes an act of constitution: the address animates the subject into existence' (1997b, 25). And yet it seems important to emphasize, as Althusser certainly does, that this representation of 'initial conditions' as a serial unfolding of events is an impossible conceit. As he explains:

> Naturally for the convenience and clarity of my little theoretical theatre I have had to present things in the form of a sequence, with a before and an after, and thus in the form of a temporal succession ... But in reality these things happen without any succession. The existence of ideology and the hailing or interpellation of individuals as subjects are one and the same thing. (1971, 174–5)

This temporal condensation where the call which has yet to be received has always/already[1] been heard has related implications for our understanding of power and subjectivity. Superficially it appears that the coercive imperative in subject formation derives from the state and is manifested in the policeman, the anonymous instrument of authority who enacts power *over* the subject. In this model, power operates as an external force that commands the individual's obedience. However, if power is truly alien to the individual before its enforcement then the individual's compliant confirmation of power's intention (to subject him) would not be possible. The subject's response, whether motivated by guilt or by something more mysterious as Althusser surmises, is evidence of a social conscience. And the existence of this 'conscience', an intuitive social knowledge that presumes a sense of belonging, is an articulation of power's 'calling to account'.

In a sense then, this scene of interpellation doesn't really require two people, or the temporal separation of before and after. To better understand this complication we can return to the struggle between Hegel's master and slave, a struggle that implicated the dynamic of inter-subjectivity with intra-subjectivity and confused the temporal distinction between initial and final conditions. The infection in Hegel's dialectic compromises any appeal to a discrete and autonomous entity, whether that entity is an individual subject or single event, because every identity secretly incorporates the difference against which it defines itself. With this in mind, we can see why Althusser's policeman need not be seen as a separate subject who pre-exists the one who responds or, indeed, as someone whose action corresponds to coercion. If we view the policeman as an Everyman then the call is inseparable from the response; indeed, a response is already presumed in the call's intention and, in a sense, evokes it. Given the intimacy of this implication, power isn't an external force that is pitted *against* the subject in this account because it is the internal algorithm of the subject's possibility and transformation. In other words, if the subject is already power's reflex, its object and agent, then power is not an instrumental or repressive tool of subordination that bears down upon its victims.

Althusser's thesis that the Ideological State Apparatus (ISA) is realized *in* the subject presumes that there is no easy escape from ideology: the independence of social institutions, personal beliefs and actions is more apparent than actual.[2] Accordingly, power's operation can be seen as somewhat tautological, a cross-referenced weave of repetition, constitution and confirmation, where the different sites of power's 'taking hold' seem to anticipate each other. For example, the specific beliefs or ideas of the subject will be manifest in the actions s/he performs and, in turn, the practice of these actions as they express the ritual rhythms of his or her existence will be self-reinforcing and demand further repetition. As Althusser explains: '... the existence of the ideas of his belief is material in that *his ideas are his material actions inserted into material practices governed by material rituals which are themselves defined by the material ideological apparatus from which derive the ideas of that subject*' (1971, 169).

Butler is especially interested in Althusser's evocation of a divine address, 'where to utter is to create the effect uttered' (1997b, 32). To explain how this might work she notes Althusser's positive reference to Pascal's inverted explanation of religious supplication: '[k]neel down, move your lips in prayer, and you will believe' (1971, 168). Butler queries Althusser's recourse to a divine vocative to illustrate interpellation's efficacy because it suggests that the voice is *the* instrument of creative power and that its effects are compelling and immediate. However, the inaugurating moment of subject formation need not be conceived in such terms. Effects can be inherited over time and their constitutive energy can operate through discursive (other representational) channels that are perverse rather than direct. Thus, neither the subject's presence nor compliance is a necessary requirement of interpellation, for a subject can be named in his or her absence, just as a subject can actively reject a name rather than own it. Butler has two seemingly conflicting points to make here: first, 'the name wields a linguistic power of constitution in ways that are indifferent to the one who bears the name' (1997b, 31); and second, 'One need not know about or register a way of being constituted for that constitution to work in an efficacious way … a chain of signification … exceeds the circuit of self-knowledge. The time of discourse is not the time of the subject' (1997b, 31).

Butler revises aspects of Althusser's scene of subject formation, especially this sense of the call's immediate recognition/efficacy, by drawing on aspects of J. L. Austin's speech act theory. In *How To Do Things With Words* (1975) Austin questioned philosophy's tendency to think of language as descriptive (constative) statements or reports *about* the world, reports whose truth or falsity could then be verified. Austin's approach shifted the terms of the discussion entirely by insisting that language was itself an instrument of social action that could realize effects and produce truths whose validity derived from the speech act itself. To explain this, Austin discriminates several different types of utterance, among them illocutionary and perlocutionary speech acts. Butler's gloss is that the illocutionary 'are speech acts that, in saying do what they say, and do it in the moment of that saying'. The perlocutionary 'are speech acts that produce certain effects as their consequence; by saying something, a certain effect follows. The illocutionary speech act is itself the deed that it effects; the perlocutionary merely leads to certain effects that are not the same as the speech act itself' (1997b, 3). In the former case the contractual statement 'I bet', when said by a gambler to a croupier, or the declaratory statement 'I do', when said in a marriage ceremony to a celebrant and future spouse, respectively constitute the fact of betting and marrying. The actual practice of language can here be described as truth producing. But language can also change events outside a specific moment of utterance. As Austin explains, a perlocutionary act can bring about con-sequences 'such as convincing, persuading, deterring, and even, say, surprising or misleading' (1975, 109).

The delay and undecidability that make it difficult to assess the effects of certain speech acts is of interest to Butler because she questions the instrumental power and efficiency attributed to hate speech by those who demand its legal prohibition. Put simply, what makes an utterance successful and can its effects be firmly established? What ingredients will guarantee that the intention to wound has hit home? According to Austin, the effectiveness of an utterance can only be ascertained in terms of the 'total speech situation', but he admits that there are difficulties in determining the parameters of this event. For example, we can readily understand why a perlocutionary utterance such as a misleading statement may have ongoing consequences that can't be evaluated because the speech situation in this instance extends into the future. However, an illocutionary speech act that 'performs its deed *at the moment* of the utterance' (Butler 1997b, 3) seems comparatively straightforward because the effects of the act are easily circumscribed. Yet even in the latter case Butler queries this certainty by underlining the ritual nature of any speech situation, the historicity or convention of discursive proprieties that enable an utterance to work. By taking this more comprehensive sense of contextual performativity into account, Butler argues that *all* speech acts, even illocutionary utterances, are indefinite in some way: there is 'a life of discourse that exceeds the subject's own temporality' (Butler and Bell 1999c, 166). In other words, if the workability of an utterance will always recall past circumstances and implicitly evoke future ones, then the identity of the 'total speech act' is essentially elusive.

Although Austin doesn't go this far he acknowledges these same implications, namely that meaning evades immediate and faithful communication, when he explains that an utterance may be 'infelicitous' or 'unhappy' in achieving its intention. An utterance may fail to hit its mark if its primary purpose is parasitically hijacked and put to a different use. We see an example of this in a marriage ceremony that takes place within a play, because the recitation of the words 'I do' realizes a quite different outcome from its conventional one. While in this example the parasitic mimicry of its particular illocutionary intention is no secret, Austin grants that a speech act can arise in circumstances where the author's own primary purpose remains unclear. Has the speaker truly authorized or intended her words, has she been coerced into speaking or, to add a more difficult consideration which Austin doesn't canvass, can an author presume that unconscious motivations which may be disavowed or repressed at the time of speaking are not primary intentions? Austin concedes that an inherent ambiguity can attach to certain utterances which prevents the simple assessment 'that it was done or that he did it' (1975, 21), and he even allows that some utterances which take the form of the performative may lack the capacity to cause either immediate effects or later consequences. Austin's admission that utterances which seem to hit home can miss their target altogether, while in other circumstances the intentions of a speaker may prove irrelevant in assessing an utterance's performative success, has important consequences for the analysis of hate speech. What if language is not a precise instrument which sentences a docile subject to 'take on' its lesson?

In *Excitable Speech* Butler specifically interrogates the act of hate speech because although great suffering can be attributed to these injurious acts she disputes the juridical model of power which informs campaigns to stop it. Butler provokes her readers to consider, 'does understanding from where speech derives its power to wound alter our conception of what it might mean to counter that wounding power? Do we accept the notion that injurious speech is attributable to a singular subject and act?' (1997b, 50). Butler's point here is that 'the sovereign conceit' which installs a causal equivalence between the speaker's intention to wound, the actual representation of hate and the impact felt by the victim shows little appreciation of the problematic nature of communication. Further to this, this style of analysis inadvertently constitutes the victim of hate speech as a powerless object of the act, a passive recipient of injury whose incapacity renders them totally vulnerable. Lacking agency, the subject's only hope of protection is that the state will exercise its power to prohibit and police such acts.

Butler's criticism is that such activist demands for state control show no interventionary faith in the ability of 'the speech situation' to evoke other readings, actions and effects than a repetition of the original injury. In an interview with Vikki Bell, Butler explains her position:

> I think there are all kinds of reasons to stop a person when they speak such things [racist and homophobic speech] ... I think that's important. But I think a politics that begins and ends with that policing function is a mistake, because for me the question is how is that person, as it were, renewing and reinvigorating racist rituals of speech, and how do we think about those particular rituals and how do we exploit their ritual function in order to undermine it in a more thorough-going way, rather than just stopping it as it's spoken. What would it mean to restage it, take it, do something else with the ritual so that its revivability as a speech act is really seriously called into question? (Butler and Bell 1999c, 166)

For Butler, the juridical discourse of state intervention actively stymies the possibility of resignifying hate speech by 'establish[-ing] and maintain[ing] the domain of what will be publicly speakable ... publicly acceptable' (1997b, 77). In other words, an unfortunate consequence of the state's conflation of intention with effect is that it attributes hate speech with the capacity to *always* wound. Butler's provocative assertion that '*the state produces hate speech*' (1997b, 77) underlines how its victims are denied a right of reply that might deploy those same words. The victims in such cases can only appear as perpetrators, reiterating and reinforcing the original meaning and intention of the hate speech.

Given the privileging of speech in these accounts, Butler returns to Althusser's scene of interpellation to argue that, although the inauguration of the subject is linguistic, the constitutive modality of 'language' need not be confined to speech as Althusser implies. Instead, she suggests that the scene of the subject's emergence involves a discursive and representational complexity whose repetitions and recitations reverberate through an array of implicated, performative modalities. These extend outside what we might conventionally think of as a purely textualist context,[3] and their operation is not that of the divine voice which presumes to 'bring about what it names' (1997b, 32). As Butler notes, if interpellation can take place 'out of earshot, as, say, the referent of a third-person discourse' (1997b, 33), then discursive subjectivation is not the immediate and obedient response to a command. The individual could, for example, ignore the policeman's call, run away or defiantly protest the call's accuracy and its presumptive recognition. And yet Butler is not suggesting that identity can escape discursive constitution; rather, her intention is to destabilize correspondence theories of language and to complicate what is actually meant by this notion of 'discursive constitution'.

An important consideration for Butler is that the outcome of language is always threatened by incoherence, contingency and ambiguity, for it involves an intricate web of dispersed causality where the presumed integrity of authorship and authority, meaning and intention, are 'spoken through' by convention. This means that discursive convention is not a static structure but one which 'suffer[s] destructuration through being reiterated, repeated, and rearticulated'. With this in mind, Butler asks, '[m]ight the speech act of hate speech be understood as less efficacious, more prone to innovation and subversion, if we were to take into account the temporal life of the "structure" it is said to enunciate?' (1997b, 19).

In Jacques Derrida's analysis of J. L. Austin's work Butler finds a finessed explication of this repetitive, citational operation in language which destabilizes Austin's terms of reference even further. However, as Butler tries to marry the principal tenets of Austin's argument with Derrida's extensive criticism of them, certain tensions in this bricolage of approaches begin to emerge. Why Butler looks to Derrida to provide a complexity she feels compelled to qualify, and whose final implications she pointedly rejects, seems curiously misguided. Perhaps, because the proponents of hate speech legislation make positive reference to Austin and ordinary language theory, Butler is provoked to illustrate her thesis by showing how these same terms of reference might suggest radically different conclusions, and Derrida's intervention seems to realize this aim. But is the oppositional tenor in Butler's engagement with anti-hate speech legal activists sustainable when we consider that a Derridean approach will always uncover the shared and unacknowledged commitments in any opposition? If the point of Butler's intervention is to foreground interpretive play and intertextual possibility, then the conventional naysaying of critique, represented here in an argument that stands against censorship, is somewhat compromised. In other words, there is an uneasy recuperation of the politics of censorship and prohibition in Butler's own stance *against* censorship. To explore the more counter-intuitive aspects of these questions we will need to understand why Butler justifies her rejection of Derrida's conclusions about how language works in terms of the more pressing, political realities of everyday life. Does deconstruction really eschew such pressing concerns?

Derrida's argument, an argument that will undo the easy distinction between straghtforward meanings that hit their mark and more wayward, ambiguous ones, takes its leverage from what Austin excludes or marginalizes as 'anomaly, exception, "non-serious," *citation* ... or rather, a general iterability' (Derrida 1988a, 17). Derrida will insist that the logic which distinguishes these so called 'exceptions' is also constitutive of the very possibility of *any* performative, because the very intelligibility of language derives from repetition and contextual difference. In 'Signature Event Context' (1988a), Derrida subsumes the enabling structuration of any performative utterance to the breaking force (*force de rupture*) of a written sign. This means that any purported entity, whether a sign, a speech act, an individual intention or specific context, will be 'hailed' by the force of repetition and re-contextualization, a force whose historicity and contingent implications rupture identity *from the inside*. As we will see, this is a crucial point that both Austin and Butler move over much too quickly. To explain what is at stake here, Derrida notes that Austin's examples of performative failure and infelicity liken the risks or 'traps' 'into which language may *fall* or lose itself' to external threats, threats which seem to '*surround* language like a kind of *ditch* or external place of perdition' (Derrida 1988a, 17). For Derrida, however, these fault lines are internal to every aspect of language because there is no originary coherence which pre-exists this 'breaking up' of the language operation.

Importantly, Derrida generalizes the structural condensations and interruptions that make language work to all modalities of experience and expression (1988a, 9), and this seems to support Butler's intervention against the phonocentric privileging in Althusser's scene of interpellation. But Derrida's 'generalization of language' is no simple extension, if by this we mean that other perceptual modalities or discursive performatives can also be included, or, given this logic, that speech need not be present at all. Butler's critique of phonocentrism attributes a specific identity to the voice which leads her to assume that perception is an aggregation of quite different modalities that can be either present or absent. However, Derrida's generalization of language aims to destabilize this way of thinking which segregates perception into separate ciphers. According to Derrida, what is needed is not so much a bringing together of stand-alone capacities (to hear, to touch, to see, and so forth), as it is a recognition that each 'one' is *already* synaesthetically entangled. As we will return to this point, suffice it at this stage to note Butler's helpful gloss on Derrida's overall argument. '[A] performative "works" to the extent that *it draws on and covers over* the constitutive conventions by which it is mobilized. In this sense, no term or statement can function performatively without the accumulating and dissimulating historicity of force' (1997b, 51).

Armed with a battery of analytical methodologies, Butler's task becomes something of a juggling act. To recapitulate, she asserts that language does exercise the force of an action upon an addressee and it has the capacity to register material effects, to wound and to injure. Yet she also maintains that language exerts no *direct* or causative imperative upon subjects as the proponents of hate speech legislation believe. Given these seeming contra-dictions, coupled with their theoretical abstraction, she provides several concrete examples of injurious speech acts to give her analysis pragmatic purchase. Although the particular instances of racial, homophobic and misogynistic violation she chooses are specific to the US context and its legal intricacies, they carry more general relevance and application. As space permits only a selective representation of some of the assumptions which attend just one of these case studies, what follows is a critical assessment of why Butler opposes the legal regulation and censorship of pornography.

Pornography in its various forms is regarded as hate speech by several of its better-known academic opponents.[4] For example, Catharine MacKinnon, a legal philosopher and anti-pornography activist, imbues words and images with a power that Butler describes as 'efficacious, unilateral, transitive, generative' (1997b, 74). To liken pornography to an illocutionary speech act is to assume that the delivery of its injury is immediate. It also assumes that pornography will *always* result in the political reinscription of woman's inferior status. Butler recognizes these same assumptions in the legal scholar Mari Matsuda's position, which insists that:

> ... speech does not merely *reflect* a relation of social domination; speech *enacts* domination, becoming the vehicle through which that social structure is reinstated. ... hate speech *constitutes* its addressee at the moment of its utterance; it does not describe an injury or produce one as a consequence; it is, in the very speaking of such speech, the performance of the injury itself, where the injury is understood as a social subordination. (Butler 1997b, 74)

If we assume that there is no space for contestation then the demand for government protection against ongoing and un-avoidable harm becomes imperative.

However, Butler strongly disagrees with this conflation of representation and action, as we see in her critical examination of MacKinnon's *Only Words* (1993). Although MacKinnon regards a pornographic representation as a sign or stand-in for experience, she imbues it with what Butler regards as the 'fantastic' capacity to realize itself as an actual experience. As

Butler explains it, 'this second-order experience is rendered synonymous with a second-order "reality," which suggests that in this universe of pornography there is no distinction between an experience of reality and reality' (1997b, 66).[5] MacKinnon also broadens the notion of interpellation to include vision, a shift which Butler worries will extend the divine performative of the vocative and the immediate efficacy of its authorial command to other representational genres. But if there are problems with MacKinnon's insistence that pornography has the sovereign power to achieve its representational intention and constitute 'what a woman is', we need to consider if there are also problems, indeed, an inversion of the very same ones, in Butler's belief that 'pornography neither represents nor constitutes what women are' (1997b, 68). Unfortunately, the oppositional nature of such arguments whose twists and turns are meant to decide if language/representation either works because it means what it says (MacKinnon), or else fails because it doesn't or can't (Butler), can simply ignore or deny the ontological complexity of language/representation that enables it to incite very different, even contradictory meanings and reactions from the 'same' language event – even from the 'same' person. For example, when Butler concedes that language is undecidable, inasmuch as it always remains open to interpretation, she uses this argument to counter the very specific way it takes hold for particular people – in this case, anti-pornography activists. Yet when she rejects what she regards as Derrida's abstract generalizations about language in favour of the specificity of lived historical meanings that endure and 'stick' to people, she illustrates, albeit inadvertently, why these two positions aren't mutually exclusive. Does an argument about the open-endedness of language and meaning-making necessarily displace arguments that assume meaning is congealed and seemingly static?

It should now be apparent that Butler's analysis of hate speech locates the possibility of interpretive political transformation in what she conceptualizes as a break in the circuitry of significa-tion, a gap whose dislocation *re*-signifies. Locating and under-standing what we might call the technology of the negative, this apparently empty space where so much can happen, remains the enduring political objective in Butler's work. In the reflexive disjuncture of Althusser's interpellative *mise-en-scène*, in the infelicity and delay of Austin's perlocutionary, and in the iterative reinvention of Derrida's citationality, we are offered several approaches which together reinvigorate 'the performative' and undermine the sovereign stamp of meaning and identity. Butler also deploys a Foucauldian approach to power which disperses its presumptive concentration throughout the body politic, rendering the subject a product of its 'manifold forms' rather than the helpless object of its sovereign constraint. In the latter case, what is important is that the break or gap of difference thought to separate the powerful from the powerless is diffracted and generalized in a way that implicates all of us in power's ontology.

Noteworthy in Butler's reference to Foucault is that the sovereign sense of domination which power's distributed 'self-involvement' reconfigures isn't radically rearranged. Instead, the sense of repression is retained and pluralized as the 'manifold forms of *domination*' (Foucault, in Butler 1997b, 79: emphasis added) which enable the microphysics of power's restrictive energies. Butler endorses Foucault's call to interrogate:

> ... how things work at the level of on-going subjugation, at the level of those continuous and uninterrupted processes which subject our bodies, govern our gestures, dictate our behaviours etc. ... we should try to discover how it is that subjects are gradually, progressively, really and materially constituted through a multiplicity of organisms, forces, energies, materials, desires, thoughts, etc. We should try *to grasp subjection in its material instance as a constitution of subjects.* (Foucault, in Butler 1997b, 79)

In this instance, the *dispositif*, or mechanism of power, is 'continuous and uninterrupted' and should not be confused with the subject itself. Indeed, it is in the 'radical incommensurability' (1997b, 28) between them that Butler secures their ontological difference and the possibility of change.

And yet it is hard to reconcile this particular representation of Foucault with the theorist who encourages us to consider that power doesn't seize upon a body which pre-exists it, that resistance is power's *internal* reflex, and that ideas and concepts have a materializing, corporeal efficacy. Nevertheless, given the direct citations from Foucault it is fair to say that Butler can glean his support for her argument in places. However, in a good many others Foucault's contribution to the problematic of power cannot be enlisted into a surreptitious recuperation of the repressive hypothesis. The heterogeneity of Foucault's work is a perfect illustration that sovereignty, even when it is figured in the proper name, is an errant authority, a diffracted identity. For example, in the *History of Sexuality* (1980a), Foucault notes that '[d]iscourse transmits and produces power; it reinforces it, but also undermines and exposes it, renders it fragile and makes it possible to thwart it' (1980a, 101). Described as 'discontinuous segments' by Foucault, the incoherence of discourse makes it radically incapable of maintaining a single aim or intention. '[Its] tactical function is neither uniform nor stable' (1980a, 100).

Important in this description is the *inherent* ambiguity of discourse, the way it functions, *simultaneously*, as 'a point of resistance and a starting point for an opposing strategy' (1980a, 101). And yet for both Austin and Butler the sense of undecidability in power's intention or efficacy is visited upon the sign/discourse from the outside when it is subjected to the perlocutionary register of time's distortions and space's recontextualizations. Indeed, what Austin calls an 'infelicity' and Butler deems a 'failure' mark the loss of the sign's original identity/integrity. However, Foucault's contribution to the performative uncovers a multiplicity of force relations *within* the sign/discourse which would certainly question the sovereignty of its identity from the start.

Butler's theoretical commitment to a prelapsarian plenitude before the fall is the organizing trope which explains the structural instability of power/knowledge/language in terms of the failure to access, and be anchored by, the in-itself of reality before its re-presentation. Or, if we remain within the supposed circumscription of language/representation/culture, it becomes the failure to receive the integrity, or truth of the sign's original meaning before its corrupting reiteration. This original purity returns in a different guise when Butler opposes radical, resistant discourses/practices, which actively invite contestation, to conservative or compliant ones which foreclose and prohibit it. But why should the identity of anything be defined in sovereign terms as *either* repressive *or* resistant? As we saw in the earlier discussion of Hegelian dialectics, oppositional differences can be more apparent than actual, a point exemplified in Butler's subtle recuperation of an argument she eschews elsewhere.

To explain this further, Butler disagrees with MacKinnon's investment in the sovereign efficacy of the performative because she is persuaded by 'the Foucaultian view that contemporary power is no longer sovereign in character' (1997b, 74). The juridico-discursive or sovereign view of power separates the state from the citizenry as if the population is power's hapless object. Countering this, Foucault argues that power is a dispersed network of relational forces and the *raison d'état*, or 'art of government', is exercised *by* the population rather than over and against it. In other words, governmentality is a complicitous circuitry wherein the population is both power's resource as well as its target. Governance involves knowledges and practices enacted by populations in their struggle to organize themselves. Thus, given the entangled nature of power's identity, the difference between resistance and repression remains provisional, fraught, always implicated and, finally, undecidable.[6]

And yet when Butler acknowledges the 'arbitrary and tactical' use of power in the courts, the sense of the law's capriciousness, errancy and contradictory expression are taken as proof of a secret consistency, or unity, in power's 'own' ruthless and reactionary intention:

> The arbitrary use of this power is evidenced in the contrary use of precedents on hate speech to promote conservative political goals and thwart progressive efforts. Here it is clear that what is needed is not a better understanding of speech acts or the injurious power of speech, but the strategic and contradictory uses to which the Court puts these various formulations. (1997b, 62)

There are two important points to be made here. First, to equate state and legal regulation with the repression of language by sovereign intent, as if the life of language is truly arrested because the state *does* contain the sovereign capacity to 'mean what it says', seems decidedly unFoucauldian. This argument also runs against the grain of Butler's more nuanced insights into power, as does her assumption that the *recycling* of hate speech in civil society should be privileged as the potentially resistant and progressive site of its subversion.[7] Butler's own description of her project makes this elision between power and state domination, at least in this instance, clear. 'My concern is not only with the protection of civil liberties against the incursion of the state, but with the peculiar *discursive power* given over to the state through the process of legal redress' (1997a, 77).

However, the more interesting, if troubling, provocations in Foucault's work refuse these neat bifurcations. As Catherine Mills explains:

> [Butler] neglects the fact that various progressive movements have been importantly assisted by state intervention. The point that is elided here, then, is that *a priori* designations of state intervention as reactionary, neutral, or even necessary, miss the vagaries of the state's position within relations of power and political contestation. (2003, 266)

Nevertheless, and this is why things remain interesting, to suggest that power is *not* sovereign and centralized doesn't *therefore* mean that Butler is misguided when she argues against state intervention in certain cases, or that MacKinnon *et al.* are foolish to demand it in others. The problem is that, because both positions attribute power with fixed and sovereign capacities which are differently held in *either* the population *or* the state, both sides remain unaware of power's complex ontology and their shared commitments.

We see this in Butler's opposition to MacKinnon *et al.* where she is forced to reject their claim that hate speech *is* injurious conduct, as if the break between expression and perception precludes this possibility; as if meaning's true intention has indeed been lost. As a result, Matsuda's unremarkable observation that words *do* 'hit the gut' (Matsuda, in Butler 1997b, 75) is met with an elaborate sophistry of denial that offers little more than a 'sticks and stones' dismissal. However, Butler's rejection of

Matsuda's point in this instance is in complete contradiction to the corporealization of language in *Bodies that Matter*. There, even gender, sex and sexuality emerged as the living, material manifestations of language and discourse, and the difference between phantasmatic idealizations of reality (which are always personal and interested) and the Real was no difference at all. *Excitable Speech*, on the contrary, is so intent on refuting the correspondence theory of language that it concedes no realizing energy to the erotic charge, as well as the pain and humiliation, of pornography. Instead, Butler represents pornography as if it is merely 'an imaginary scene', a phantasmatic fiction of 'impossible' representations, 'hyperbolic gender norms', 'uninhabitable positions [and] compensatory fantasies'. It is its failure to work that 'gives the pornographic image the phantasmatic power that it has' (1997b, 68). It seems that pornography's intention can be 'depicted' but not 'delivered' according to Butler: it doesn't hit its mark. And this difference enables 'a feminist reading of pornography that resists the literalization of this imaginary scene'. In sum then, 'if the text acts once, it can act again, and possibly against its prior act' (Butler 1997b, 69).

Although the distinction between speech acts and acts in general (conduct) seems blurred in this instance, pornography's original intention to demean is, apparently, never in question in Butler's account.[8] But why isn't the very identity of pornography, the 'what it is and how it works', already an interpellative performance of undecidability, a 'scene' that hails different readings and experiences which 'hit the gut' with pleasurable force, anger, disgust, excitement, or even indifference? In other places, Butler seems to concede that the interpellative mess of the pornographic event confounds rigid identification with any one person, one act, or one meaning (1990b, 114–15) – because, quite simply, this is how we quite 'normally' identify as subjects with otherness. Why then does Butler insist that pornography involves 'impossible positions' and 'unrealizable' scenes meant to compensate for sexual failure, as if the diversity, curiosity and robust self-exploration of a population's sexual life is radically *dis*articulated from its representations of itself? Why assume that a radical break separates people's lived realities and perceptions from representation? And why is this entangled scene of subjectivation divided as if 'with an axe' (Derrida 1984, 121) into two incommensurable parts?

If we return to Derrida for illumination here, we will recall that Austin was criticized for investing in the sovereign self-presence of the sign which consequently failed to hit its mark when wrenched from its original context. As Derrida explains it, it was as if the original sign fell from grace, as if what makes it different is this falling into the gap that '*surround[s]* language like a kind of *ditch* or external place of perdition' (Derrida 1988a, 17). Unfortunately, Butler's gloss on Derrida's criticism of Austin reinvests in the notion of difference as something which befalls a sign that was previously intact, rather than carefully explicating what might be implied by the generalization of an *originary* breaking open. The latter disrupts the notions of both failure and success which take their measure from the integrity of a prior referent. However, because Butler invests in the sign's purported failure to mean what it *once* did, she finds herself in a muddle whereby the sign's recitation (iterability, citationality) severs it from the history of convention and ritual, and therefore from the significance of its political inheritance and lived reality. By attributing this rather sterile position to Derrida, she compounds her error with several similarly misguided explanations of his work that lead her to openly acknowledge the awkward impasse that results and her need to part company with him.

To recapitulate, despite Butler's happy deployment of deconstruction in the initial phase of her argument, its rejection proves inevitable because she understands 'iterability' as the severing of context from sign. As a consequence, the ritual dimension of the performative becomes something of a problem if its political dimension has been lost. In this regard, Butler asks if 'the mark is "cut off" from its origin, as Derrida contends, or loosely tethered to it [which] raises the question of whether the function of the sign is essentially related to the sedimentation of its usages, or essentially free of its historicity' (1997b, 148).

According to Butler, Derridean performativity 'opposes the structural dimension of language to the semantic and describes an autonomous operation of the structural apparently purified of social residue' (1997b, 148), a position Butler finds pragmatically unworkable. However, when Derrida insists that '[t]here is nothing outside of the text [*il n'y a pas de hors-texte*]' (1976, 158), his generalization of the graphematic structure (the structure of relationality/difference) acknowledges a systemic implication which embraces everything: language *is* sociality at work. Indeed, the recombinant potential of 'language' is an evolving force whose self-reference ('writings') can't be reduced to the conventions of linguistics as Butler assumes, even though Derrida makes this point again and again. As he underlines: 'The concept of text or of context which guides me embraces and does not exclude the world, reality, history ... the text is not the book, it is not confined in a volume itself confined to the library. It does not suspend reference ...' (Derrida 1988b, 137).

If we agree that power and 'language' (in the Derridean sense) are consubstantial, then Butler's conceptualization of power as originally sovereign leads her to miss what is perhaps most provocative in Althusser, Foucault and Derrida. For example, if the policeman (sovereign power) is always/already both subject and object of power, then interpellation enacts the internal and eternal misfit of power's intentions. According to this interpretation, policing (domination) is essentially errant rather than a subjugating force of compliance internalized by the entire population. This reading anticipates Foucault's contribution to rethinking power's ontology as always productive, efficacious, materially constitutive and essentially perverse. And it evokes Derrida's sense of 'scribble power' (Derrida 1970) as a force-field of iterative energy and generative possibility. Unfortunately, Butler's investment in original loss opposes difference to identity, and this inability to appreciate that identity is internally ruptured (differentiated) returns like a genetic algorithm to divide Butler's argument into mutually exclusive categories: resistance versus domination, the structural versus the semantic/social, the body versus language, the population versus the state, sovereign intentions versus the perversion of their thwarted effects, the visual versus speech and writing, success versus failure, and so on. If the spirit of Butler's project is to acknowledge the enabling ambiguities of language/power so that life can be lived more robustly, more equitably, then there is no reason to reject Derrida's 'notion' of 'iterability' in order to argue this. A more pressing challenge does emerge, however, because if we grant this general impurity then the practice of criticism, which diagnoses difference, will need to acknowledge the common ground we all share with our protagonists.

Chapter 6

Identity and Politics – The Psychic Life of Power: Theories of Subjection. Undoing Gender

As we have seen in previous chapters, the familiar coordinates of analysis that stabilize investigation and guarantee the relevance of social inquiry are not as reliable as they seem. All those foundational categories and identities that we normally take for granted – the difference between nature and culture; the divisions within gender, sex and sexuality that bifurcate into mutually exclusive attributes and desires; correspondence theories of language that explain reference in terms of meaning and truth; or the adjudication of what seems oppressive from what is more enabling, or even emancipatory – all of these simple discriminations have become more provisional and certainly contestable in Butler's hands. However, one of the enduring and perhaps more awkward questions that haunts such anti-foundationalist accounts concerns the problem of agency and responsibility: how can we change our individual and collective lives for the better if we lose faith in the very terms that explain our predicament and mobilize our energies?

In this section we will consider this problem by exploring the paradoxical relationship between the subject and power and the vexed status of agency. Butler explains the contradiction that needs to be addressed:

> Many conversations on the topic [power] have become mired in whether the subject is the condition or the impasse of agency. Indeed, both quandaries have led many to consider the issue of the

subject as an inevitable stumbling block in social theory. Part of this difficulty, I suggest, is that the subject is itself a site of this ambivalence in which the subject emerges both as the *effect* of a prior power and as the *condition of possibility* for a radically conditioned form of agency.

    ... There is, as it were, no conceptual transition to be made between power as external to the subject, "acting on," and power as constitutive of the subject, "acted by." (1997a, 14–15)

Butler is concerned that when power is regarded as a separate 'property' then it seems inevitable to compare it to a commodity that can be possessed or lost, or to a force that we control, or are controlled by. Butler aims to 'steer clear' of this style of thinking because it allows only one of two possibilities – 'naive forms of political optimism' or 'politically sanctimonious forms of fatalism' (1997a, 17). In other words, an instrumental notion of the subject *vis-à-vis* power doesn't investigate the paradoxical nature of power, the 'double valence of subordinating and producing' that is internal to power (1997a, 2) and the many questions that arise from this. For example, how can power be both positive *and* negative, and what do we actually mean when we make these discriminations? Are these moral categories of good versus bad, a power that constructs and makes, versus a power that breaks and destroys? And if this is the case, is this an adequate way of comprehending the ontology of power? Can resistance *be* domination at the same time, perhaps from a different perspective? Is power bifurcated into two quite different 'intentions' or is it inherently undecidable?

    Butler gives such questions a more concrete context when she asks *how* subjectivation (the process of assuming an identity, *assujettissement*), or what we might normally gloss as the individual's socialization, is achieved. As Butler believes that the subject is 'formed in submission', her thesis explores the subject's motivation to acquiesce or 'subject himself' to power's demands. And yet, even this representation of the puzzle fails to capture Butler's intellectual fascination, because if power is defined against subjectivity then how can the subject express her individual agency and actually *be* a force (power) to be reckoned with? How can power take hold *within* the subject, inhabiting its very interiority and to such an extent that the subject's own psyche, individual will and sense of personal agency appear as manifestations of power's own purpose? What happens to the subject if there is no outside of power?

Although the subject seems erased in this description it surreptitiously reappears in the form of power's decidedly human attributions. Anthropomorphism, which discovers human capacities and characteristics in objects, animals and even natural forces, certainly haunts Butler's account, and this displacement of identity is emphasized in the book's title – *The Psychic Life of Power*. However, the resulting confusion needn't represent an erroneous attribution of properties and processes, for this reversal of capacities encourages a provocative disruption of the very terms that define the question. To impute human intention to the notion of force/power, while at the same time destabilizing the subject as a self-possessed and self-conscious agent, muddles the reference points of these debates and makes us think more deeply about our (humanist) premises. As Foucault describes the puzzle: 'Power relations are both intentional and nonsubjective ... they are imbued, through and through, with calculation: there is no power that is exercised without a series of aims and objectives. But this does not mean that it results from the choice or decision of an individual subject ...' (1980a, 94–5).

In this collection of essays Butler revisits various thinkers who explore identity by acknowledging that 'a subject is passionately attached to his or her own subordination' (1997a, 6). Themes that are now quite familiar reappear. The peculiar vacillation of power and identity in Hegel's master/slave relationship is further interrogated through 'The Freedom of Self-Consciousness: Stoicism, Skepticism, and the Unhappy Consciousness'; Althusser's scene of the subject's interpellation is revisited; and Freud's work on primary narcissism, repression and the development of a conscience, as well as the relevance of his argument to what Butler describes as 'melancholy gender', is also reviewed. However, as the overarching concern of these essays is better to understand the psychic form that power takes, Butler concentrates on bringing psychoanalytic theories of prohibition into conversation with Nietzsche and Foucault's notion of an affirmative power of production.

The book's thesis has two closely related sites of intervention. First, Butler will argue that even the most sophisticated theories of power have a tendency to evacuate the subject's interiority from the scene of subjectivation and ignore the relevance of the psyche in this process. Her answer to this oversight is to show why a Freudian, or psychoanalytic, approach represents a valuable supplement to these theories and an important component in the conceptualization of agency. Indeed, Butler's insistence that the process of subjectivation is *not* reducible to subordination will exercise her critical attention. As she describes her argument's foundational premise:

> Agency exceeds the power by which it is enabled. One might say that the purposes of power are not always the purposes of agency. To the extent that the latter diverge from the former, agency is the assumption of a purpose *unintended* by power, one that could not have been derived logically or historically, that operates in a relation of contingency and reversal to the power that makes it possible, to which it nevertheless belongs. That is, as it were, the ambivalent scene of agency, constrained by no teleological necessity. (1997a, 15)

Returning now to the second point of intervention, this concerns the way we differentiate the social – those political norms and regulations that appear to us as outside and prior to the subject – from the psyche, the self-affection that is inside, seemingly consonant with the subject, and logically resistant to alienation. In order to reconfigure the scene of political contestation and individual agency in more robust and effective ways, Butler will open the division between the psyche and the political to the same strategic revisions she brought to the nature/culture, material/representation distinction. We already have some insight into the sort of temporal and spatial dis-order that occurs when 'initial conditions' turn out to be retrospective, or second-order constructs (for example, where nature is revealed as a cultural sign), and we are also aware that such reversals can inadvertently recuperate the very same problems they strive to resolve.

What we will need to determine is how closely Butler's argument follows these previous manoeuvres and, if so, whether this presents similar points of tension that might qualify her overall project. The following clear description of her concerns, as well as some helpful hints about their representational ambiguities, provide us with a useful departure point:

> Is the [social] norm first "outside," and does it then enter into a pre-given psychic space, understood as an interior theater of some kind? Or does the internalization of the norm contribute to the production of internality? Does the norm, having become psychic, involve not only the interiorization of the norm, but the interiorization of the psyche? I argue that this process of internalization *fabricates the distinction between interior and exterior life*, offering us a distinction between the psychic and the social that differs significantly from an account of the psychic internalization of norms. (1997a, 19)

As the discussion of these issues must be selective, it seems appropriate to concentrate on 'Subjection, Resistance, Resignification: *Between Freud and Foucault*', because this particular theoretical encounter offers an instructive representation of what Butler is trying to achieve. However, as a preliminary caution it is worth underlining that Foucault's representations of power and the subject, when considered across his entire oeuvre, are riven with discrepancies and outright contradictions. We saw clear evidence of this in the last chapter, and these confusions reappear in this essay as Butler moves between his various writings, seeming to endorse the value of one approach only to counter and then reject its commitments with another. Importantly, this positional 'stuttering' is a self-conscious strategy on Butler's part, meant to negotiate the minefield of inconsistencies in Foucault's work and in a way that will do something more interesting than merely diagnose them. As these twists and turns are deliberately disorienting we will need to pay close attention to their consequences.

The argument begins with the opening scene from Foucault's *Discipline and Punish* (1982), where a fascinated crowd witnesses the annihilating force of juridical law. In this spectacular illustration of corporeal punishment all eyes are on the prisoner.

And yet there is much more going on than the unfortunate victim's slow and calculated torture at the behest of sovereign will. Although the nature of power as pure domination seems unequivocal in this instance, Butler reminds us that power is intransitive – it has no object. In certain of his writings Foucault is quite specific on this point, reversing power's direction and evoking a sense that power springs from the ground itself, from what we might otherwise perceive as its (power*less*) object: '[p]ower comes from below; that is, there is no binary and all-encompassing opposition between rulers and ruled at the root of power relations, and serving as a general matrix' (1980a, 94). For Foucault then, power doesn't reside in a central point, 'in a unique source of sovereignty from which secondary and descendent forms would emanate' (1980a, 93). Instead, power is generalized and its identity dispersed and fragmented like a network or force-field, and these flows of energy and their different intensities are immanent in all social relations. In sum, '[p]ower is everywhere; not because it embraces everything, but because it comes from everywhere' (1980a, 93).

What we hear in these descriptions is something decidedly counter-intuitive, because Foucault is undermining the equivalence between power and control. As a consequence, the causal logic that allows us to determine the origin of power and its direction is also undone, because if every cause is already an effect then even the prisoner is power's agent. To cite Foucault again, 'power must be understood in the first instance as the multiplicity of force relations immanent in the sphere in which they operate and which constitute their own organization' (1980a, 92). But what are we to make of such confusing claims? How should we anchor and assess them? Butler helps us here by explaining that power's ambivalence is centralized through the body. In the torture of Damiens, the regicide, his body becomes the site and sign of transgression and culpability but also the site that sanctions rituals of normalization (1997a, 83); perhaps we could even risk the suggestion that it invites them. However, there is a definite sense in Butler's interpretation that power is, first and foremost, negative, restrictive – a unitary force that originates outside the subject and stamps it into submission:

[S]ubjection is a kind of power that not only unilaterally *acts on* a given individual as a form of domination, but also *activates* or forms the subject. Hence, subjection is neither simply the domination of a subject nor its production, but designates a certain kind of restriction *in* production ... with the prisoner it is clear that the subject produced and the subject regulated or subordinated are one, and that compulsory production is its own form of regulation. (1997a, 84)

Although this description acknowledges an internal differential *within* power, an ambivalence that moves between restricting and producing, 'production' in this instance remains synonymous with the capacity to render controllable. In other words, power is a constraining force that subordinates so effectively that it even 'activates' (produces) its object *as an object to be subordinated*. Now, although Foucault quite vehemently distances himself from such conceptualizations of power in some of his writings (and we catch a sense of this from the citations above),[1] it is also true that in other work, indeed, work such as *Discipline and Punish*, he seems to encourage the rather dismal view that power's reflex *is* a comprehensive microphysics of sovereign will and domination. Quite clearly, this doesn't sit well with an argument that disperses power's identity, not just its range of controlling operations but its very identity, throughout the entire social body to include all its relations and expressions. In the latter position, the generality of power's 'productivity' *is* the relational dynamic of sociality itself – or what we might describe as the myriad torsions of sociality's 'self-reflection' and re-production.[2] Power can't be equated with constraint in this account, although it would include it; rather, it is an expression of the inherent differences that enable society to be itself, to obtain knowledge of itself (power/knowledge), to engage with itself and transform itself through every registration of its self-encounter. Butler doesn't adopt this reading however, because her question is framed in terms of the 'formative or generative *effects* of restriction or prohibition' (emphasis added). Consequently, the fact that power is conflated with prohibition *in the first instance* isn't the issue under review, so much as the variable nature of prohibition's outcome – its unpredictable, perverse and sometimes positive results.

We will need to consider this interpretation as our 'guiding thread', at least as a provisional stratagem, as it will help us negotiate the maze of Foucault's contradictory assertions about power and the implications of Butler's interested reinterpretation of them. What we are aiming for is a better understanding of what is at stake in these debates and why Butler is right to want to reconfigure their terms. To take up this thread then, given Butler's commitment to a disciplinary notion of power *in the first instance*, it makes sense that her driving aim will be to find a way around it that will illustrate how power fails to realize its (controlling) intentions. To this end, she concentrates on Foucault's neglect to explain *how* power comes to inhabit the subject's interiority, rendering him docile. Foucault makes reference to the subject's interiority in his description of the Panopticon, a prison whose architectural arrangement incorporates such observational efficiency that it allows the prisoner no privacy. But 'no privacy' is a misleading description in this instance, because the prisoner's secret life, his inner dreams and desires, are not so much thwarted by his imprisonment as they are constituted and affirmed. In other words, his personal interiority is so effectively inculcated with disciplinary expectation that he *is* the psychic instrument of his own compliance – 'he becomes the principle of his own subjection' (Foucault 1982, 203). Foucault eschews psychological explanations of this process and elides its actual operation by focusing on the totality of its outcome, using the word 'soul' to evoke power's effectiveness in seizing the very core of the subject's being. As Butler explains it:

> ... the soul is figured as itself a kind of spatial captivity, indeed, as a kind of prison, which provides the exterior form or regulatory principle of the prisoner's body. This becomes clear in Foucault's formulation that 'the man described for us, whom we are invited to free, is already in himself the effect of a subjection [*assujettissement*] much more profound than himself ... the soul is the prison of the body.' (1997a, 85)

Because Butler perceives that this metaphor of incarceration has general application in Foucault's overall theory of subjectivation, she has several points to make in this regard. First, she argues that Foucault's evocation of the subject's 'soul' and its 'imprisoning frame' assumes more than it can explain, and she suggests that a psychoanalytic account offers important insights into how power actually takes hold. Second, and more importantly, Butler believes that a psychoanalytic elaboration of subject formation represents a much less totalizing and deterministic view of the subject because it demarcates the normative demands of the Symbolic order from the de-regularizing eccentricity of the individual's psyche, or unconscious. In other words, because the unconscious exceeds power's normative conventions its operations are inherently resistant to power's demands. Thus, instead of Foucault's rather disheartening suggestion that the interiority of the body is the unilateral effect of disciplinary power, Butler will argue that the psyche's internal dissonance and resistance represents a space whose transvaluations might help us conceive 'a radically conditioned form of agency' (1997a, 15). And yet Butler remains dissatisfied, for as we have come to expect, there is much more to the story than a little psychoanalytic repair work to Foucault's conception of power can resolve. Nevertheless, with the value of psycho-analysis now conceded, at least provisionally, Butler will turn her critical attention from Foucault to psychoanalysis: she will find a more radical use for the Foucauldian terms she has just rejected, and a more troubling set of implications in the psychoanalytic argument she has just embraced.

In order to understand this second 'stage' of Butler's meditation on the subject and agency we need to remember that a consistent signature in her intellectual methodology is a rigorous attention to 'initial conditions' – to a place, a time, a primordial substance, state of being or, in this case, a state of mind – that is said to precede or exceed normative regulation and symbolic intelligibility. For this reason, Butler is not persuaded by the state of freedom and autonomy afforded the psyche. As she explains the problem:

> If the unconscious, or the psyche more generally, is defined as resistance, what do we then make of unconscious attachments to subjection, which imply that the unconscious is no more free of normalizing discourse than the subject? ... What makes us think

that the unconscious is any less structured by the power relations that pervade cultural signifiers than is the language of the subject? If we find an attachment to subjection at the level of the unconscious, what kind of resistance is to be wrought from that? (1997a, 88)

On a different yet related note (and it is one that informed Butler's criticisms of Kristevan abjection and gender formation), Butler asks what radical leverage can be gained by acknowledging that the psyche exceeds the demands of the Symbolic order if the very nature of its difference from the Symbolic prohibits it from actually changing its terms. The incapacity of the psyche to effect political change offers little comfort, because '[e]ven if we grant that unconscious resistance to a normalizing injunction guarantees the failure of that injunction fully to constitute its subject, does such resistance do anything to alter or expand the dominant injunctions or interpellations of subject formation?' (1997a, 88).

Although the possibility of reconfiguring a more robust notion of agency now seems frustrated, Butler returns to Foucault's axiom that nothing exceeds power in order to wring a more hopeful interpretation from it. In Foucault's curious notion of the soul, the instrument which allows power to actualize, or bring the body into being, Butler hears an echo of Aristotle's formulation that the soul is the 'form and principle' of corporeal matter. But whereas previously the soul seemed to mark the impossibility of resistance within power's disciplinary apparatus it now heralds its inevitability, albeit via a circuitous route. Butler reminds us that in Foucault's disciplinary notion of power objects can only be said to 'materialize' – that is, appear as identifiable, knowable, liveable – because they are the actualized investments of power. And if materialization is coextensive with this investiture then the body's material reality can't be independent of this process: indeed, there can be no body before this investiture, before this inscription.

But there is some equivocation in Foucault, because although the soul seems to enframe and become the body in *Discipline and Punish*, in other writings there is a very definite sense that an untrammelled body pre-exists power's capacity to inscribe it.[3]

This isn't surprising, as the very description of the soul as power's instrument engenders such a reading. However, Butler has little interest in showing the lapses in Foucault's argument at this point, instead drawing our attention to the interesting relationship between several analytical 'categories' that appear as different temporal 'moments' and spatial configurations in this process – namely, the soul, the subject and the body. In Foucault's 'Nietzsche, Genealogy, History' (1984), for example, Butler notes that the body's material presence seems to fade, displaced by a subject whose very emergence 'appears at the expense of the body, an appearance conditioned in inverse relation to the disappearance of the body' (1997a, 91–2). Butler is quite deliberate in her use of a psychoanalytic vocabulary to explain this process:

> The subject not only effectively takes the place of the body but acts as the soul which frames and forms the body in captivity. Here, the forming and framing function of that exterior soul works against the body; indeed, it might be understood as the sublimation of the body in consequence of displacement and substitution. (1997a, 92)

To reclaim some possibility of an agential space of non-compliance that exceeds the injunction of obedience, Butler needs to interrupt the unilateral efficacy of power's subjectivating force in some way. And in this blurring of the subject with the soul an interruption does emerge, inasmuch as both 'processes' seem to be exteriorized outside the body.

> The body is not a site on which a construction takes place; it is a destruction on the occasion of which a subject is formed. The formation of this subject is at once the framing, subordination, and regulation of the body, and the mode in which that destruction is preserved (in the sense of sustained and embalmed) *in* normalization. (1997a, 92)

If the soul is the normalizing ideal through which the subject assumes coherence *as* an embodied subject, *in* a body whose identity is specularized and discursively regularized into social legibility (an ideal, an imago), then Butler surmises that the body that enables this process continues to endure in some way, even though it is sublimated *within* the process of normalization. Happily then, things are not frozen into place, as if normalization is a straightforward process that can be finessed once and for all. Sublimation must constantly be reinstated and maintained, and this means that the subject is always in the process of coming into being within the shifting valencies of social reinscription. Although the reference here is to Nietzsche, we are reminded of *Excitable Speech* and the transformational effects of performativity. As Butler explains it, because the sign's original intention is perverted and changed when read through a different context, meaning and truth are always provisional, unstable and in need of repair to re-establish their standing, their authority. If this structural stutter in power's operation is truly intrinsic to subjectivation, then the subject's mandatory subordination to power is never a process of docile compliance.

At this juncture Butler makes an interesting observation between psychoanalysis and Foucault: in the former, the subject (of the Symbolic) is differentiated from the psyche (the interiority of the individual that exceeds social regulation), and in the latter the subject, or soul, emerges from a body that enables subjectivation while somehow preceding and exceeding its injunctions. Butler muses that perhaps the Foucauldian body and the psychoanalytic psyche have interchangeable functions, but how might this blurring of terms prove suggestive for a more radical appreciation of identity and agency?

If power is haunted by the ghostly residue of the body, something it can't shake off, then the psychic life of power incorporates an internal disjunction that does two things at once: on the one hand, it incites a performative iteration of norms in order to reinstate their authority and, on the other, this very repetition derails the possibility of power's unilateral efficacy as a purely dominating force. In other words, there will always be a 'misfit', some sort of interruption between the demand to conform and the individual's capacity to faithfully comply. And this rewriting, or rerouting, marks the ambivalence and perversion that *is* the psychic life of power.

This emphasis on power's inherent incapacity to realize its

intention is significantly different from the representation of disciplinary power as 'the efficacy of the symbolic demand, its performative capacity to constitute the subject whom it names' (1997a, 97). And it is also very different from socialization theories that struggle to explain the psychic internalization of norms. Because if Butler is right in her suggestion that 'this process of internalization *fabricates the distinction between interior and exterior life*' (1997a, 19), then she has radically shifted the terms of the debate in several related ways. First, Foucault's axiom 'there is no outside of power' implied that subject formation was forged through the disciplinary structures of a prison house, where docility proved inevitable as there was no escape. However, Butler has taken that same axiom as proof that power's teleological intention to render the subject totally compliant is impossible. Second, she has questioned the psychoanalytic axiom that the psyche is anterior to power (the social) and therefore radically incapable of rewriting the letter of the law: in her reformulation, the psyche doesn't simply thwart or resist the law – it actively transforms it because it inhabits it. And if the psyche is internal to power then power's identity is inherently unstable – indeed, we might describe it as 'constantly different'.

By calling on representations of power from *The History of Sexuality*, representations which emphasize that power is 'formative or productive, malleable, multiple, proliferative, and conflictual' (1997a, 99), Butler argues that this 'multiplicity of power vectors' can't be accommodated within a juridical understanding of the law. Consequently, the psychoanalytic notion of the Symbolic order, the regime that forces compliance to social demands, is opened to a constitutive dis-order, a contestatory politics wherein 'the law itself is transmuted into that which opposes and exceeds its original purposes' (1997a, 99).

Yet having established this more open-ended sense of political possibility, and with it the suggestion that individual agency emerges out of the performative interruptions of the law, that is, from *within* the interstices of power's myriad dispersed and competing vectors, Butler seems to pull back from these implications. We are returned to a Foucault who worries about the repression of the citizen by the state, a citizen whose very subjectivity exemplifies a 'kind of individuality which has been imposed on us for several centuries' (Foucault, cited in Butler 1997a, 101). Concerned by the effective repression of this 'historical hegemony' and the reduction of the subject to 'plaintiff status', the Foucault who affirms the repressive hypothesis encourages us to 'refuse what we are ... [an identity] which is the simultaneous individualization and totalization of modern power structures' (Foucault, cited in Butler 1997a, 101). However, Butler is critical of Foucault's emancipatory gesture here, not because she disagrees with the repressive notion of power that motivates it, but because the voluntarism in Foucault's invitation ignores the subject's erotic attachment to the identity categories s/he inherits. Regardless of their painful injury, identity designations aren't extraneous abstractions that can be thrown aside because we feel burdened by them: we assume an identity, a meaning, an interior life, *through* such names and their significance, and not in spite of them.

How Butler gets us out of this apparent impasse by returning to Freud's work on primary narcissism and the development of a conscience has been discussed at length in a previous chapter. Suffice it to say here that *because* desire and the law are inextricably intertwined, and because the law will always fail to realize its aim (to render normative, to make proper, to fit an ideal), Butler argues that things must change: our erotic lives can be reconfigured and our identities transformed as the law strives to re-establish itself. Importantly, the 'residue' of this performative misalliance represents an agential space of reinvention where identity is reconstituted. This is the substance of Butler's response to the emancipationist tendencies in Foucault (we can't simply evade the law), as well as to his seemingly bleak vision about the unilateral effectiveness of power. In other words, the law's intention is constantly thwarted and this process interrupts the seamless actualization of pure prohibition and passive conformity.

But let us recall that Foucault's 'strategic' perspective is neither emancipationist nor defeatist and, given this, why should we recommit to this notion of the state as a 'transcendent singularity' of repressive force when it seems unlikely that power's identity could ever have been a unified, unilateral expression of domination?[4] A corrective proves difficult here when we consider that Foucauldian arguments about the repressive ontology of power can always be parried against Foucauldian arguments about its affirmative force as a tactical, strategic, mobile and ubiquitous energy. Because these are radically different perspectives the justification for their respective adoption is perhaps more interesting than any adjudicatory appeal to Foucault himself might hope to resolve. In sum then, the first representation of power is, from the start, a prohibitive authority, commodified by ruling elites and institutions. But in the second scenario, where power is a relational force-*field* of shifting intensities, alignments, consolidations and dispersals, power has no *one* purpose or coherent identity – no teleological aim. In the latter case, to describe power as comprehensive doesn't mean that repression is totalizing.

Butler's clever engagement with the puzzle of power certainly encourages this radical reterritorialization of affirmative energies. However, her foundational commitment to a juridical notion of power seems to qualify the more exciting directions in her argument, leaving us with a battery of questions. Why, for example, must we assume that power's *primary* intention is to control and sublimate the pre-discursive body and enforce its normalization? Or, even if we are persuaded by this claim, why must we accept that power's (pure) intention to dominate endures despite a 'psychic life' that guarantees errancy, deviation and unforeseen possibilities? How, or why, would power return to an original determination, a strictly 'normative purpose', if its identity is forged from the disequilibrium that inhabits *all* social interactions? We might recall that Foucault describes power as 'everywhere; not because it embraces everything, but because it comes from everywhere' (1980a: 93). Within this strategic sense of power, the identity of a norm, or even the law, would be an involved one. For example, if a norm arises from the myriad vectors of negotiated intercourse that enable a population to reproduce itself (for good and bad), to 'rub up against itself', then norms will evolve accordingly and instantiate a population's strategies of existence. A norm might be likened to an entire society's 'mirror stage' imago, its ideal form, where the very process of this self-reflection, this self-regulation, authors a norm's lived necessity as well as its contingency.

Norms reconsidered

Seven years later, in *Undoing Gender* (2004a), Butler broaches these questions about identity, vulnerability and agency with a refreshed eye. The signature themes in her work reappear in the book's subject matter and their methodological treatment, and yet the question of identity holds more fascination in these essays. The frame of analysis takes on a 'social science' feel, with rigorous attention to empirical data, institutional practices and the historical contexts that inform contemporary political struggles. And while such close reference to pragmatic detail is hardly new, the philosophical purchase in these essays appears more grounded and alive to the broader anthropological questions that haunt the human condition.

Questions about gender identity and sexuality become even more ambiguous as Butler acknowledges the challenges from the 'New Gender Politics', a 'combination of movements concerned with transgender, transsexuality, intersex, and their complex relations to feminist and queer theory' (2004a, 4). But this recognition that the landscape of gender politics is now significantly reorganized doesn't undermine Butler's previous position: it actually illustrates it. Because her enduring commitment is to explain why gender identity is always troubling, impossible and yet necessary for all that, these more recent acknowledgements of gender experience provide further evidence of the contingencies that inform, entangle and inevitably compromise *all* identity claims. For this reason, Butler questions the adjudicatory impetus in a lot of gender activism and argues for a more generous and less acrimonious frame of discussion:

> The task of all these movements seems to me to be about distinguishing among the norms and conventions that permit people to breathe, to desire, to love, and to live, and those norms and conventions that restrict or eviscerate the conditions of life itself. Sometimes norms function both ways at once, and sometimes

> they function one way for a given group, and another way for
> another group. What is most important is to cease legislating for all
> lives what is livable only for some, and similarly, to refrain from
> proscribing for all lives what is unlivable for some. (2004a, 8)

A change that does emerge from these essays, and we see it in
the previous comment, is a more enlivened questioning of what
we mean by norms and normative power. Previously, normative
power was equated with pure constraint. Indeed, the signature of
a norm's purely repressive intention was evidenced in its
remarkable ability to reconsolidate this intention even after its
purpose had been thwarted and transformed. Because the
coherence of this inaugural repression was assumed, Butler was
forced to introduce resistance in the form of a *later* temporal
moment that could iterate (re-form, rewrite) that initial demand.
In an earlier chapter, however, we noted that Derridean iteration
infects meaning, identity and intention *from the start*, and it is this
undecidable condensation wherein many outcomes are realized *at
the same time* that Butler now concedes to normative power.

In the essays 'Gender Regulations' and 'The Question of
Social Transformation', norms appear synonymous with the
patterns of behaviour and comportment that a society takes for
granted – unconscious grids of intelligibility. Although they may
be explicit 'they usually remain implicit, difficult to read,
discernible most clearly and dramatically in the effects that they
produce' (2004a, 41). Put simply, norms enable social life. But
where previously they were likened to ideal models – inaccessible
imagos of social propriety and achievement – they now appear as
the quotidian stuff of bodily ritual and social intercourse. As
Butler's aim is better to understand how the actual action or
practice of everyday, normative behaviours might provide
opportunities for change, she draws on the work of two theorists
who specifically address this question. Indebted to Foucault, the
sociologist François Ewald argues that a norm's common
standard is abstracted from a society's self-referential involve-
ments. Somewhat like the evolving implication of a semiological
system, it operates as a sort of 'difference engine', generating
change from within: 'What is a norm? A principle of comparison,
of comparability, a common measure, which is instituted in the

pure reference of one group to itself, when the group has no relation other than to itself, without external reference and without verticalit' (Ewald, cited in Butler 2004a, 51).

Within this self-enclosure, aberration doesn't arrive from the outside: it is an effect that emerges from the relational condensations of social interaction. As Ewald goes on to explain:

> The abnormal does not have a nature which is different from that of the normal. The norm, or normative space, knows no outside. The norm integrates anything that might attempt to go beyond it – nothing, nobody, whatever difference it might display, can ever claim to be exterior, or claim to possess an otherness which would actually make it other. (2004a, 51)

However, if opposition to the norm derives from the norm, Butler worries that this particular interpretation of Foucault will appear depressingly similar to Lacan's notion of the Symbolic order; in other words, the *radical* resignification of norms will be impossible. At this point Butler turns to Pierre Macherey, who reprises an earlier point about power's intransitivity, its 'self-possession', to move the argument forward. Describing his intervention as a 'thesis of immanence', Macherey explains that we need to shift the terms of analysis from a 'mechanism of determinism' that conceives power in causal terms, acting on things, to a more involved understanding of power's internal relationality. If it is 'the relationship which defines the action of the norm', then:

> ... this relationship is not a relationship of succession, linking together separate terms, *pars extra partes* ... but it supposes the simultaneity, the coincidence, the reciprocal presence to one another of all the elements which it unites. From this point of view it is no longer possible to think of the norm itself in advance of the consequences of its action, as being in some way behind them and independent of them; the norm has to be considered such as it acts precisely in its effects – in such a way, not so as to limit the reality by means of simple conditioning, but in order to confer upon it the maximum amount of reality of which it is capable. (1992, 186)

We hear a resonance here with Saussure's struggle to explain the consubstantiality of the sign, recalled in Derrida's notion of 'iteration', where the sense of an 'other', an 'again', is already present *within* the sign, the sentence – a generality that underpins identifiability. This problematic is also reminiscent of the Hegelian system and its peculiar 'totality', where every *one* is also plural, and the horizon of transformation is universally 'present'. If the norm is an immanence within a field of application, this is because it produces that application, that action, and within that action it produces itself (Macherey 1992, 187). Macherey hears the biological momentum in this description of an originary imma- nence, and reminds us that Spinoza regarded the state of nature and the state of society as continuous. What Macherey gains from this enlargement of 'the political' is that when norms become 'necessary and natural' they forfeit their claim as fixed templates of regulation: if they are not defined against anything then they are more accurately considered as evolving patterns of systemic self- reference that express the interactions of an entire population.

Two things should be explained here. First, Butler's analysis of power forecloses the origin, and this foreclosure mandates power's iteration as a failure to achieve its (repressive) intention. As we have seen throughout Butler's work, and despite its considerable sophistication, her analysis will always commit to a juridical notion of the law that is incapable of maintaining itself. However, in Macherey's 'natural model' of normative immanence there is no presumptive foreclosure, prohibition or absolute loss that drives power's attempt to affirm itself. In other words, whereas Butler requires a sense of failure to guarantee an agential space of contestation that allows the mutability of norms, Macherey discovers what we might call 'an immanence of agency' in power's self-affirmation: in other words, power's *essential* incoherence and productive proliferation mean that change is constant.

The second point that should be emphasized is that, despite the significant differences between these theorists, Butler does deploy this sense of power's dynamic interiority to further refine her conception of subjectivation. For example, she argues that gender identity isn't something that must approximate a timeless and inalterable ideal:

If gender is a norm, it is not the same as a model that individuals seek to approximate. On the contrary, it is a form of social power that produces the intelligible field of subjects, and an apparatus by which the gender binary is instituted. As a norm that appears independent of the practices that it governs, its ideality is the reinstituted effect of those very practices. This suggests not only that the relation between practices and the idealizations under which they work is contingent, but that the very idealization can be brought into question and crisis, potentially undergoing deidealization and divestiture. (2004a, 48)

What is significant in this reading is that if the law is never indifferent to what it regulates then even abjected genderings arise from *within* normative power and, in their turn, are effective in reproducing the law otherwise. A logical extension of this argument that evokes semiological condensations is that 'a complex convergence of social meanings' will always be operative within any one aspect of identity formation, even if there is no specific reference to it. Butler's point is that if the scene of regularization and normative power incorporates all of society's practices and interactions, then norms are neither predetermined nor fixed.

Finally, and perhaps most importantly, Butler returns to the structural distinction between the Symbolic law and social norms, promulgated in the work of Lévi-Strauss and Lacan, where the Symbolic assumes the cross-cultural status of an 'elementary structure of intelligibility' that is indifferent to the specificity of particular social norms. As the political ascriptions that accompany these elementary structures are deemed incontestable, Butler eschews the division, and through her reading of normative immanence the Symbolic itself emerges as 'the sedimentation of social practices'. But there is a fascinating corollary to this insight that many of Butler's critics find unpalatable, and it is this. If the very ontology of power is now so comprehensive and ambivalent that it can no longer be equated with prohibition and control, then there can be no guarantee that certain forms of political activism that equate power with repression won't unwittingly abet the very conservative structures they condemn (2004a, 55). It is certainly the case that what seems conservative may indeed reveal hidden opportunities and possibilities, and vice versa. But if there is an increasing sense of uncertainty and hesitation about 'what should be done' to promote a more equitable and generous understanding of human potential one has the sense that Butler is happier to work with the difficulty than to deny it. This isn't a gesture of political paralysis but one that encourages us to consider the contexts of our decisions in their broadest possible terms.

Chapter 7

Butler on Others – Others on Butler

For those of us with a passion for scholarly research the throwaway comment 'it's all academic!' feels especially pointed. After all, it's not really a description meant to acknowledge the conceptual difficulty in our specialist expertise; it's more a perfunctory dismissal of its relevance. In an anti-intellectual climate the scholar may be more tolerated than valued when the commerce of intellectual life fails a clear-talking reality test. Explanations abound. There is a sense that intellectuals are social misfits with neurotic research obsessions that hide their social incapacity. As marginal figures they seem out of touch and their propensity for developing private languages as they struggle to explain themselves tends to keep things that way. Among the colleagues of these sorry figures who can't communicate is another caricature: the intellectual who deliberately contrives to enhance her self-importance with élitist jargon. But such negative judgements of incapacity, hubris and downright irrelevance are remarkably inconsistent, for the target of these prejudices seldom hails from the sciences: it is never the physicist or the medical researcher who faces attack because they explain the nature of reality in arcane terms.

The difference in trust and respect conceded to certain research areas and withheld from others rests on the community's perception of their comparative usefulness. And with the commercialization of universities in a global market and the commodification of knowledges as priced options, the devaluation of critical thinking in the humanities seems inevitable.[1] After all, what can you actually *do* with all that rumination?

Unfortunately, the need to reflect on the conceptual architecture that makes a world meaningful will seem precious and unnecessary if the weight of reality and its political exigencies are regarded as self-evident, and this is the precise reason why the style of critique that Butler undertakes can provoke such anger and exasperation. Its stated aim is trouble-making. It *intends* to cause discomfort, 'to bring into relief the very framework of evaluation itself' (Butler 2004c, 307), to unsettle the ideological grammars that confer significance. Its nuisance value is inexhaustible because there is no reassurance at the end of this questioning, no promise of resolution that will still the uncertainty. Anticipating her critics, Butler asks 'what good is thinking otherwise, if we don't know in advance that thinking otherwise will produce a better world?' (2004c, 307). But it is the simple conviction that there is general agreement about what this better world will be that illustrates her point, namely, that there are 'sure and already established standards' that make certain possibilities unthinkable. This means that Butler's compulsion to question this foreclosure will require some unusual manoeuvring to say the least; an oblique approach that will '[put] at risk the field of reason itself' (2004c, 311) and, with it, what we mean by a political and ethical practice.

Not surprisingly, the reception of Butler's prolific contribution to theoretical and political life depends on the importance attributed to such concerns. However, for those who appreciate the associated difficulties that *must* attend it – the sometimes awkward expression, the tendency towards ambiguity and open-ended conclusions, the technical terms and so on – there is a readiness to perceive the business of interpretation as a working opportunity to redefine the field of value and possibility. For others, however, the difficulty can be put down to 'bad writing', and Butler is routinely accused of this by those who denigrate certain styles of political and theoretical criticism, and by other academics, often on the left, who regard the use of 'alienating language' as an abrogation of social responsibility.[2] Butler's rejoinder is two-pronged. In response to the demand that her argument be transparent and accessible and its difficulties clarified, she notes:

It's not that I'm in favor of difficulty for difficulty's sake; it's that I think there is a lot in ordinary language and in received grammar that constrains our thinking – indeed, about what a person is, what a subject is, what gender is, what sexuality is, what politics can be – and that I'm not sure we're going to be able to struggle effectively against those constraints or work within them in a productive way unless we see the ways in which grammar is both producing and constraining our sense of what the world is. (2004b, 327–8)

Further to this, Butler conjectures that attacks from people in the humanities about the relevance of her work and its mode of expression are symptomatic of a deeper anxiety:

... people in the humanities no longer know whether they're central to the academy; they know that they're derided by the outside, and they don't know how to articulate how their work can have concrete effects on the lives of the students and the world in which they live ... Those intellectuals who speak in a rarefied way are being scapegoated, are being purged, are being denounced precisely because they represent a certain anxiety about everyone's effect – that is, what effect are *any* of us having, and what effect *can* we have? ... the persons who are being scapegoated probably remind the scapegoaters too much of their own dilemma. (2004b, 329)

The most notorious criticism of Butler's purported verbal opacity and political irrelevance comes from the philosopher of law and ethics, Martha Nussbaum. In a vitriolic outpouring in *The New Republic*, Nussbaum attacks Butler's scholarship as flimsy and its political influence as dangerous, a 'hip quietism' that 'collaborates with evil' (1999, 13). Butler is thoroughly demonized as a person who eschews hope. '[W]hen a major theorist tells women in desperate conditions that life offers them only bondage, she purveys a cruel lie, and a lie that flatters evil by giving it much more power than it actually has' (1999, 11).

As the fervour in these accusations suggests, Nussbaum's argument is morally shrill; its tone is one of outrage and its insults are aggressively personal. And given her opening confession that 'it is difficult to come to grips with Butler's ideas, because it is difficult to figure out what they are' (1999, 2), her inattention to their detail is surprising. Where Nussbaum does engage, her representations are such misleading cartoons that her criticism has little purchase. Indeed, by the end of the article it becomes clear that Nussbaum's scratchy invective has more to do with professional *ressentiment* than it does with intellectual disquiet.

As Nussbaum places no credence in the actual value of Butler's insights she is forced to explain their relative success in mysterious terms. Consequently, Butler is attributed with magical capacities, inveigling her readers with a sleight-of-hand obscurity that seduces 'scores of talented young women' into abandoning 'a sense of public commitment' (1999, 13). By sarcastically describing this style of work as 'sexy' no less than four times in the article, Butler takes on the mythical powers of a Jezebel cum Pied-Piper of Hamlyn. Her influence is not explained in intellectual terms but in a tone one might reserve for a charlatan, someone who can mesmerize an audience and, in this case, lead a significant number of contemporary readers to abandon concrete politics in favour of 'fancy words on paper' (1999, 1).

The irony, however, is that it is Butler who painstakingly defends the view that there are many ways of doing politics, many ways of being a feminist, and that the concrete activism of community struggle and debate is inseparable from academic argument. In the crucible of social exchange and interaction all forms of activism, and this includes writing, nourish and cross-reference each other. There is no ivory-tower abstracted from everyday experience, nor is there one raw and brutal 'coal-face' that can determine 'what is to be done' across the entire fabric of political life. The spirit of Butler's contribution is evident in its strategic intervention and mode of debate. Although she disagrees passionately with other theoretical commitments and political positions, nowhere does she revert to a moral argument that simply denounces her protagonists because they hold different viewpoints. Her crime, it seems, is her suspicion of those who do. In a passing comment on Nussbaum's attack, Butler muses:

> I think it actually has nothing to do with my work. ...I presume that it does probably epitomize a certain frustration that a certain

kind of liberal American politics has with a critical approach to some of its most important issues. She wants to be able to make strong paternalistic claims about women's conditions; she wants to be able to use the language of universality without interrogating it ... We can see something like a resurgence of a certain kind of white feminism here that doesn't want to have to hear about difference, that wants to be able to make its strong claims and speak in the name of 'reason,' and speak in the name of *everyone* without having to hear them, without having to learn what it might mean to hear them. (2004b, 356)

This minimal rejoinder refuses the sort of vicious crossfire that one might expect in such circumstances, perhaps because Butler appreciates the broader considerations that frame her response. How, for example, should we practise criticism and critique? Are there ethical considerations in the very way we go about foregrounding our own position, and is it necessary to denigrate another's in the process? The structural bifurcation that automatically renders an 'other' deficient (as we have seen with 'Nature', 'woman', 'the ethnic and racial other', 'the homosexual' and so on) is also at work in an argument's dialectical logic. In a very real sense, then, if the formal vehicle that enables us to mount an argument is as value-laden as its actual subject matter, then it behoves us to consider these more subtle political inflections within our practice.

In 'What is Critique? An Essay on Foucault's Virtue', Butler addresses this question specifically, noting how things 'become more vexing if we attempt to distinguish between a critique of this or that position and critique as a more generalized practice, one that might be described without reference to its specific objects' (2004c, 304). Concerned with this same problematic, Raymond Williams worried that criticism was too often restricted to mere 'fault-finding', and he warned against the intellectual complacency that can hide behind a rush to judgement (2004c, 304). Theodor Adorno expressed similar disquiet, believing that an effective intellectual praxis that is fully immersed in the social world can never transcend that situation and pretend to offer a disinterested judgement. In her gloss on the value of this discussion, Butler provides a useful perspective on her own project: 'Judgements operate for [Williams and Adorno] as ways to subsume a particular under an already constituted category, whereas critique asks after the occlusive constitution of the field of categories themselves'. Through an elaboration of Foucault's contribution to this same question, she emphasizes the importance of 'try[ing] to think the problem of freedom and, indeed, ethics in general, beyond judgement: critical thinking constitutes this kind of effort' (2004c, 305).

By investigating the relationship between certain epistemological formations and power, or what Williams called 'uncritical habits of mind' and Adorno understood as ideology, Butler discerns that the object of criticism is the shifting grammar of normativity. As she explains it, the obstacles, limits and constraints that arise from certain tried and true ways of knowing actually inspire or produce critique. In other words, critique doesn't simply oppose norms from a position outside their influence, it actively responds to the 'tear in the fabric of our epistemological web', where 'entire realms of unspeakability' begin to challenge our comprehension (2004c, 308). However, if the intellectual is at something of a loss when faced with this discursive impasse (because to some extent she is documenting her own uncertainty), Butler discovers something positive in the honesty of the exercise. With Foucault as her guide she explains his distinction between an ethics of obedience, where the good citizen follows the rules and regulations of a society, and an ethical practice that risks the unknown:

> For Foucault, critique is 'a means for a future or a truth that it will not know nor happen to be, it oversees a domain it would not want to police and is unable to regulate.' ... this exposure of the limit of the epistemological field is linked with the practice of virtue, as if virtue is counter to regulation and order, as if virtue itself is to be found in the risking of established order. ... He writes, 'there is something in critique that is akin to virtue.' (2004c, 308)

It would be inconsistent with Butler's understanding of the individual as a social artefact, a subject whose very being is articulated by social rules and precepts, if she explained the disobedience that a critical practice implies in terms of 'the innate freedom of the soul' (2004c, 313). Still working with Foucault, she dilates on this notion of freedom by insisting that it can't be reduced to voluntarism for we can't choose simply to ignore or overturn normative demands. Rather, a critical practice is forged *within* the mangle of power/knowledge as the validity of absolute limits is negotiated. Although we are all bound by social rules and normative constraints we interpret and experience these constraints differently. For example, a particular normative demand (assuming we could isolate such a thing) might feel like a burdensome humiliation for one person and a positive force of self-affirmation for another. Thus, the viability of these imperatives is an operational exercise that is subject to negotiation, manipulation and transformation. Put simply, norms are articulated and re-formed by the population that lives them.

It is worth lingering a little longer over this matter, as it will explain Butler's recalcitrance in the face of critics who reprove the unusual mode of her political practice as well as her equivocation about the goals and outcomes that normally motivate political activism. The extraordinary breadth and volume of Butler's writing about a great many political concerns surely attest to her enduring commitment to social change. However, the style of 'immanent critique' she adopts does prevent 'recourse to a more fundamental political or moral order' (2004c, 312), and this lack of a sure foundation means that the ground of her argument is forged from 'the horizon of knowledge effects within which it operates' (2004c, 313). This attempt to *in*-habit an argument by mining the structures of its authorization can unsettle our initial assumptions, even those that distinguish a conservative argument from a more politically generous one. However, it is by risking the certainty in our adjudications and looking for alternative resources in places that seem to foreclose them that unusual and innovative perspectives are engendered. That there are dangers in this strategy is obvious, as Butler fully acknowledges:

> How does one call into question the exhaustive hold that such rules of ordering have upon certainty without risking uncertainty, without inhabiting that place of wavering which exposes one to the charge of immorality, evil, aestheticism? The critical attitude is

not moral according to the rules whose limits that very critical relation seeks to interrogate. But how else can critique do its job without risking the denunciations of those who naturalize and render hegemonic the very moral terms put into question by critique itself? (2004c, 313–14).

We have seen Butler's vigilant interrogation of the politics of truth in regard to 'What counts as a person? What counts as a coherent gender? What qualifies as a citizen? Whose world is legitimated as real?' and so on (2004c, 314). Importantly, these investigations acknowledge a power/knowledge nexus whose manifestations appear in all social relations – from the most personal of behaviours, interactions and claims of individual identity, to the larger structures of state and economic organiza-tion. As the politics of truth are determined through well-accepted patterns of regulation, grammars of the sensible and discursive frames of logic and reason, Butler maintains an enduring attention to these discursive structures; after all, the very process of subjectivation proceeds through these grids of intelligibility whose logic dictates 'what will count as a life' (2004c, 321). And it is for this reason that Butler insists that these conceptual and discursive modes of production/evaluation be recognized as important sites of political contestation.

But what difference can this monitoring of norms hope to achieve if we remain bound by them? Butler answers her critics by drawing on Foucault's argument in *The Use of Pleasure* (1986), an argument that contemplates the ethics of self-fashioning, or how we might transform ourselves by way of the very norms that seem to constrain our lives. As Butler understands the strategic nature of this 'ethical questioning ... [it] requires that we break the habits of judgement in favor of a riskier practice that seeks to yield artistry from constraint' (2004c, 321). And so we see that what may appear as a rather abstract set of concerns with no real bearing on concrete politics may actively enable quite significant and subversive outcomes.

Judith Butler's prolific contribution to contemporary critical and post-structural theory is now so widely read and debated that certain facets have become part of the vernacular in this field of scholarship. Such notions as 'Butlerian performativity', the

signature way Butler explores the sex/gender/sexuality distinctions, as well as other social processes of identity formation and
normativity – all these are important and familiar reference
points for anyone who undertakes research in these areas.
Perhaps her achievement in this is her ability to offer readers
the sort of provocative nourishment that enables many and
varied perspectives, even ones that express their disagreement.
Among them, one could note Cheah (1996), McNay (1999),
Dollimore (1996), Hood-Williams and Cealey Harrison (1998),
Bordo (1993), Mills (2003), Campbell (2005) and many others.[3]
But for all their criticisms, all of these writers approach Butler's
work in the spirit of its writing, that is, as food for further
consideration rather than as a template to be either followed or
dismissed. A rather amusing comment by Dollimore, who has
serious misgivings about Butler's reading of homo/heterosexual
melancholy, captures this general appreciation of Butler's
contribution, even when, at least to this critic, it seems 'hopelessly
wrong'. Commenting on her assertion that 'the "truest" lesbian
melancholic is the strictly straight woman, and the "truest" gay
male melancholic is the strictly straight man', Dollimore remarks
that '[t]his is of course such a theoretically exquisite irony that it
seems churlish to wonder whether it is true' (1996, 537). Perhaps
Dollimore's point is that it offers such an inventive conceptual
assault on our received understanding of sexual identity, and in a
way that is difficult to put aside, that it is something to be
welcomed.

Given the detailed discussion of Butler's approach and
commitments in the previous chapters, it becomes easier to
anticipate her response to the various concerns of her critics. As
space is prohibitive we will look briefly at just two examples of
these exchanges in order to gain a sense of what is at stake in
these encounters. First is Nancy Fraser, whom Butler values for
the 'productive disagreement' in their ongoing dialogue (2004b,
355). In *Feminist Contentions: A Philosophical Exchange* (1995a),
they collaborate with Seyla Benhabib and Drucilla Cornell in
an important four-way conversation about each other's work:
this fertile exchange has since been sustained across several
publications.[4] Like Butler, Fraser has no love of 'false

antitheses', and for this reason she questions the bleak economy
in Butler's understanding of subject formation that seems to
mandate exclusion. As Fraser sees it:

> ... in Butler's view, the constitution of a class of authorized subjects
> entails 'the creation of a domain of deauthorized subjects, pre-
> subjects, figures of abjection, populations erased from view.'
>   But is it really the case that no-one can become the subject of
> speech without others' being silenced? Are there no counter-
> examples? ... Is subject-authorization *inherently* a zero-sum game?
> (1995a, 68)

Not unrelated to this concern about the structural segregations
that seem to organize or validate Butler's commitments, Fraser
worries that Butler's focus on performativity and linguistic
resignification cuts her adrift from the 'everyday ways of talking
and thinking about ourselves ... Why should we use such a self-
distancing idiom? What are its theoretical advantages (and
disadvantages)? What is its likely political impact?' (1995a, 67).
Building on these misgivings, Fraser remarks that Butler's use of
language can be unnecessarily esoteric, and she underlines her
concern about intellectual abstraction and disengagement by
asking why Butler doesn't concretize her demands and justify
their validity in more positive terms:

> ... in Butler's usage the term 'resignification' carries a strong, if
> implicit, positive charge. In this respect, 'resignification' functions
> in her discourse as 'critique' has been functioning in mine. But in
> another respect the two terms differ sharply. 'Critique' is logically
> connected to the concepts of warrant and justification, so its
> positive connotations are rooted in a claim to validity. This is not
> the case, however, with 'resignification.' (1995a, 67)

Fraser's point is simply stated: 'Why is resignification good? Can't
there be bad (oppressive, reactionary) resignifications? In opting
for the epistemically neutral "resignification," as opposed to the
epistemically positive "critique," Butler seems to valorize change
for its own sake and thereby to disempower feminist judgement'
(1995a, 68).

Fraser wants Butler to commit, to justify her position and validate her judgement in no uncertain terms. For Fraser, such public validations are the necessary stuff of political activism, and proof of this necessity can be found in Butler's own work, where she privileges certain theories and social practices as 'progressive or emancipatory' while judging others 'politically insidious' (1995a, 68). According to Fraser, Butler's work suffers from an attenuated conception of what will constitute an emancipatory alternative, and this refusal to envision how we might forge more liberated 'cultures of solidarity' means that her work can seem removed from real life struggles. Such oversights, in Fraser's opinion, are an inevitable result of Butler's over-attention to language at the expense of the material contingencies and intractable political obstacles that inform our daily lives.

Although the exchange is detailed, at the core of Butler's rejoinder is an emphasis on the politics of valuation, precisely because decisions about ' "what is possible," "what is liveable," "what is imaginable" are constrained in advance, and maybe in some very politically consequential ways' (2004b, 355). Indeed, as all of Butler's work testifies, the difference between language and material reality is a question to be considered rather than a fact to be discerned.

The difference between Fraser and Butler is especially evident in a more recent exchange. In *Justice Interruptus* (1997a), Fraser separates what is properly economic from what is cultural, and this leads her to the conclusion that homophobia derives from cultural discriminations which have nothing to do with political economy. As Butler glosses this position in 'Merely Cultural':

> Homophobia, [Fraser] argues, has no roots in political economy, because homosexuals occupy no distinctive position in the division of labour, are distributed throughout the class structure, and do not constitute an exploited class: 'the injustice they suffer is quintessentially a matter of recognition,' thus making their struggles into a matter of cultural recognition, rather than a material oppression. (1997c, 271)

As the title of Butler's critique suggests, she worries that Fraser has diminished the materializing effects of culture and foreclosed the very definition of 'the political' as a result. In 'Heterosexism, Misrecognition and Capitalism: A Response to Judith Butler' (1997), Fraser insists she has been misunderstood. She rejects the suggestion that she sees 'sexual oppression as less fundamental, material, and real than class oppression', or that she wants to 'subordinate struggles against heterosexism to struggles against workers' exploitation' (1997, 279). So what is really at stake in the debate between these two old friends?

Fraser's clarification of her actual position is instructive inasmuch as it inadvertently illustrates why Butler's intervention is both important, and yet so often misconstrued. Fraser explains that:

> ... central to my framework is a normative distinction between injustices of distribution and injustices of recognition. Far from derogating the latter as 'merely cultural,' the point is to conceptualize two equally primary, serious, and real kinds of harm that any morally defensible social order must eradicate ... In my conception, therefore, misrecognition is an institutionalized social relation, not a psychological state. In essence a state of injury, it is analytically distinct from, and irreducible to, the injustice of maldistribution, although it *may* be accompanied by the latter. (1997, 280)

Butler's reply is an excellent illustration of immanent critique inasmuch as her intervention redeploys the same analytical terms that explain Fraser's position, but with an interpretive difference. Butler reminds us that even Marx and Engels encouraged an expanded understanding of 'political economy', arguing that 'the 'mode of production' needed to include forms of social association as well' (1997c, 271). Butler also calls on feminist socialist argument from the 1970s and 1980s, arguments that:

> ... sought not only to identify the family as part of the mode of production, but to show how the very production of gender had to be understood as part of the 'production of human beings themselves,' according to norms that reproduced the heterosexually normative family ... The scholarship in the 1970s and 1980s sought to establish the sphere of sexual reproduction as part of the *material* conditions of life, a proper and constitutive feature of political economy. (1997c, 271–2)

For Butler, it is clear that systems of signification aren't supplementary to economic and political imperatives. Thus, even when Fraser clarifies her position by insisting that questions of signification and recognition are equal with economic concerns about distribution, and that both are primary considerations, Butler wants to foreground the very question of 'value' that subtends Fraser's analytical discriminations while remaining invisible. Butler has reiterated her commitment to this position *vis-à-vis* Fraser in more recent comments (2004b, 355).

A sustained acknowledgement that 'the problem of language [is] essential to the formulation of an anti-totalitarian, radical democratic project' (2000b, 1) is certainly in evidence in the three-way conversation between Butler, Slavoj Žižek and Ernesto Laclau in *Contingency, Hegemony, Universality: Contemporary Dialogues on the Left*. All three scholars move comfortably inside post-structuralist theorization and the philosophical traditions that inform it, and an attention to Marx as well as Antonio Gramsci's notion of hegemony, one of the organizing motifs of the book, is foregrounded. Yet despite these shared foundations and a readiness to explore their 'post-Marxist' implications, what is plainly illustrated is just how open-ended a text can be that it can evoke such different interpretive commitments. Importantly, this has been the enduring theme in Butler's work, namely that the labour of reading/writing involves an inventiveness that can provide us with different political perspectives and possibilities. The stated hope that drives the exchange is that it 'recasts (and retrieves) philosophy as a critical mode of inquiry that belongs – antagonistically – to the sphere of politics' (2000b, 4). Given this, we should not be surprised that the debate, which is certainly passionate and even heated at times, demonstrates the importance of detail.

We have seen something of Butler's disagreement with Žižek in a previous chapter, and these same differences are elaborated here. Very briefly, Butler's major concern is that if we understand the 'incompleteness of subject formation' in terms of 'static or foundational' structures, as Lacan seems to do in regard to the Real and the phallus, then we have no way of addressing how 'the subject-in-process is incomplete precisely because it is constituted through exclusions that are politically salient' (2000b, 12). For Butler, any analysis of what is normative in hegemonic structures must hold some sense of optimism, some sense that structures are historically articulated and open to mutation:

> Precisely because the transcendental does not and cannot keep its separate place as a more fundamental 'level,' precisely because sexual difference as transcendental ground must not only take shape within the horizon of intelligibility but structure and limit that horizon as well, it functions actively and normatively to constrain what will and will not count as an intelligible alternative within culture. (2000b, 148)

Žižek's rejoinder, and Laclau concurs to a large extent, is that Butler misinterprets Lacan, in particular, by confusing antagonism with opposition and radical foreclosure. When Butler accuses Žižek of configuring the Real as an ahistoricial transcendental that is untouched by the Symbolic, he returns the accusation:

> So my basic answer to Butler ... is that, with all the talk about Lacan's clinging to an ahistorical bar, and so on, *it is Butler herself who, on a more radical level, is not historicist enough*: It is Butler who limits the subject's intervention to multiple resignifications/ displacements of the basic 'passionate attachment,' which therefore persists as the very limit and condition of subjectivity.

As Žižek sees it, Butler thinks 'it is possible to resignify/displace the symbolic substance which predetermines my identity, but not totally to overhaul it, since a total exit would involve the psychotic loss of my symbolic identity' (2000b, 221–2).

This question of 'the transcendental' haunts all of the exchanges – as either the error that motivates their accusations or, just as powerfully, as the departure point and justification for their defence and counter-claim. Thus, there is something ironic in these reflections, where for every position and concern that is mounted, a 'return to sender' swiftly follows. How should we decide between them? How to adjudicate their criticisms? If we have understood anything of Butler's generous way of reading a text and her call for more considered forms of critique, then we might look for ways to delay the adjudication by fully engaging the implications of these reflections. Perhaps Butler is entitled to have the last word here: '... what it means to function as a "critical" intellectual involves maintaining a certain distance not – as Marx would have it – between the ideality of philosophy and the actuality of the world – but between the ideality of the ideal and the givennness of any of its modes of instantiation' (2000b, 269).

Chapter 8

Butler Live

Kirby: A consistent theme in your work is a rigorous attention to 'initial conditions' – those inherited logics and assumptions that authenticate certain behaviours and modes of being while denigrating others as perverse and improper. As these political prescriptions are invariably naturalized in some way, the question of nature and its purported determinations is an enduring one. In this regard, you consistently remind us that what we perceive as nature, biology or the palpable flesh of our bodily existence is always a sign that we've interpreted, a sign whose historical and cultural inheritance makes it politically contestable. But then another question arises. Don't we recuperate the mind/body, nature/culture split and its conservative political legacies all over again if we argue that culture is radically incommensurable with whatever precedes it, whatever produces it, whatever is somehow 'attached' to it? After all, it must be in the nature of biology to interpret, to theorize, to read and write. If we consider feminist psychoanalytic work on hysteria, for example, we learn that the body can somatize cultural signs and be a sign. And one thinks of Freud here, puzzling over 'that mysterious leap from the mind to the body'. In contemporary criticism there is little or no attention to how this leap, if it is a leap, is achieved. Could you expand on this difficult question for us?

Butler: I think perhaps mainly in *Gender Trouble* I overemphasize the priority of culture over nature, and I've tried to clear that up in subsequent writings, but surely there is much to be thought through here. At the time of *Gender Trouble*, now sixteen years ago, it seemed to me that there was a cultural use of 'natural' arguments to provide legitimacy for natural genders or natural heterosexuality. But that criticism did not take account of a nature that might be, as it were, beyond the nature/culture divide, one that is not immediately harnessed for the aims of certain kinds of cultural legitimation practices. I think that perhaps I started to undo this argument in *Bodies that Matter* when I suggest there that the relation between the body and discourse (of course, a different pairing than nature/culture) is one in which discourse cannot fully 'capture' the body, and the body cannot fully elude discourse. This formulation was meant to open up a space of slippage in which neither theories of natural determinism nor accounts of cultural constitution could claim a unilateral or prior place to one another. And though they are, as it were, inter-implicated in one another, they are not fully determining.

Of course, the turn from a discourse on 'nature' – itself perhaps overburdened with anachronism – to one of biology is significant. And I think we can see in work such as Anne Fausto-Sterling's, efforts to come up with 'interactive' models that insist that (a) biology conditions cultural life and contributes to its forms, and (b) cultural life enters into the reproduction of our bodies at a biological level. My sense is that her formulation is resonant with my brief effort to establish a kind of chiasmic relation between the two. After all, she also eschews forms of determinism, either cultural or biological, and yet refuses the collapse of the categories into one another.

As for the wonderful phrase that you offer from Freud on hysteria, namely, that the body can become a sign, this opens up the domain of somatization, one that is quite crucial and which, I know, has been ably addressed by feminists as diverse as Elizabeth Wilson and Elizabeth Bronfen. My own work has perhaps moved in the direction of Jean Laplanche in this regard, emphasizing the ways in which primary and traumatic impressions come to structure through iteration the trajectory of desire itself. The fact of human permeability is crucial to understanding how a 'sign' – something said, something done – can not only impress itself upon the body, but become a constitutive part of the body. In Laplanche, what is understood as 'in' the body is precisely an externality, so that the Other becomes constitutive of bodily formation. One would have to rethink the notion of 'stylizing' the body in light of traumatic formation and somatization, and I am all in favour of such a project.

Kirby: You recently commented that your earlier work on melancholia and sexual identity has been misconstrued as a developmental narrative; as if 'first and foremost there is a homosexual love, and then that love becomes repressed, and then heterosexuality emerges as a consequence'. Your disarticulation of the Oedipal triangle's heterosexual premise is invaluable. But can we avoid the tendency to align certain erotic dispositions with temporal 'moments'? The very notions of mourning and melancholia seem to retrospectively discover them.

Butler: I think that we perhaps need story-lines, but that we should treat the narrative sequence implied by such stories along the lines of allegory. After all, allegory emerged precisely as that genre that tried to give a temporal account of a set of otherworldly referents that are, by definition, outside of temporality. I would not say the exact same thing about sexual development narratives, but I think that when we speak about stages, we are making use of narrative techniques to describe a sexual formation that never does leave any of those stages behind. In the sense that infancy is itself always recurring, that no adult is finally 'over' his or her childhood, so sexual development does not precisely leave one stage for another. The last stage is folded into the next, and the last survives in some way, if only spectrally.

The point about telling the Oedipal story differently is to open up the possibility that primary attachments can take many forms. It makes no sense to assume that a girl's primary attachment will be either to the mother or to the father; it could be to both or to another caregiver, and it could be to any of these irrespective of gender. So how do we understand the normativity of those explanatory developmental models that impute a singular attachment at the beginning?

What is interesting about the psychoanalytic story is that both the putative boy and the putative girl attach first to the mother and then a set of displacements and substitutions follow. So within its own terms, a homosexual attachment on the part of the girl has to be overcome, and this constitutes the famous 'double-wave' of repression. I take this story not as true, but as a way of allegorizing the place of homosexuality for the story of normative heterosexual development. Within the narrative requirements of that story, homosexuality must be (a) primary and (b) repressed, and both of these for the girl alone. So within its own terms, this homosexuality must not only be lost, but refused, and so becomes a constitutive site of melancholia. Now, I don't take the narrative to be 'true' in the sense of corresponding to what actually happens, but I do take the narrative to be 'stipulative' in the sense that it communicates a set of norms, and is part of the process through which those norms are inculcated. Of course, the inculcation of norms does not 'work' in any automatic sense, but we can see here the way in which even the normative account of the emergence of heterosexuality presupposes a melancholia over a lost and unavowed homosexuality. I would suggest that it does not just 'presuppose' it temporally, but enjoins it, stipulates, institutes this very melancholia insofar as the narrative itself bespeaks a normative injunction to heterosexuality. In this sense, the developmental narrative has to be understood as part of a broader nexus of power and discourse.

Kirby: Your close reading of *Antigone*, together with the essays on structures of kinship and the incest taboo, represent a significant contribution to some of the most difficult themes in social theory and anthropology. It's easy to assume that the sorts of social condensations in these 'structures' only apply to 'traditional societies', or that their relevance has faded with the complexity of urban social life and its myriad arrangements. But these exceptionally provocative essays draw on the best of anthropology to revivify its terms with contemporary and political relevance. Could you talk about the sorts of concerns that motivated this work. And do you think it might prove helpful in effecting policy changes for social justice?

Butler: My sense is that many people consider kinship studies to be over, and of course there are good reasons to forfeit 'kinship studies' for all the reasons that David Schneider and others have detailed. But is that, then, the end of kinship? The problem, as I understand it, is that a conventional approach to kinship within anthropology believed that kinship arrangements could be formally systematized, and that this systematic description enjoyed a relative autonomy from other social organizations of life. Lévi-Strauss also detailed the 'elementary' structures of kinship, and though he designated these structures as primitive, he also insisted that they continue to haunt and structure contemporary life, and so by 'elementary' he also seemed to mean 'fundamental' and 'recurring'.

I am quite sure that one can dispute or, rather, must dispute the claims of kinship studies to be systematic, autonomous, formal and fundamental to the structure of society itself. It was Foucault who, along with Gayle Rubin, insisted that the modern organization of sexuality was no longer structured by kinship relations, and of course it is right that there are now a number of overwhelming social and institutional formations in which sexuality is formed and circulated. We can certainly think about psychiatric and psychological discourse itself as part of a network of *scientia sexualis* that now provide the formative conditions of sexuality, and we can also consider shifting public/private distinctions, the reorganization and undoing of family structures, and many more such issues.

I suppose my question is, then, a relatively small one, which is perhaps, in the end, two-fold. First, when we say that kinship no longer provides the elementary structures by which to understand social organization, do we also say that kinship has no part at all in the contemporary organization of sexuality and social life? Does kinship belong unequivocally to a past, or is kinship the name of what continues also to structure us, partially and sometimes spectrally, in the midst of contemporary life? Secondly, if psychoanalysis has presumed certain structures of kinship to be invariable (and Lévi-Strauss' influence here has been less than salutary), then can psychoanalysis survive the radical reorganizations of kinship that follow from single-mothering, friends-as-kin, lesbian and gay families, blended families, extended kinship networks and kin relations formed through the juridical exigencies of immigration or deportation?

My sense is that neither kinship nor psychoanalysis can be relegated to the past, since one key way that broader social forces enter into sexual formation is through the trajectory of childhood. If we think of those 'primary impressions' by which culture takes hold of us and enters into the trajectory of our own desire, we are thinking at once about infancy and the formation of sexuality as well as the mechanisms of impingement and interiorization. I'm not clear that we can separate them.

Kirby: In *Undoing Gender* you explore the question of norms and normative power more closely than in previous work, and Pierre Macherey's meditation on Foucault figures in this significant reconceptualization. You underline that norms aren't exterior templates of conformity that regulate a population, but immanent structures of action. Macherey explores this question of immanence through what he calls 'the biological model of the norm', extending Foucault's biopower to include a 'natural history of norms', a 'force of life' that might even accommodate Spinoza's substantive sense of agency. But in your reading of Macherey you leave off at the point where this rather wild interpretation is elaborated. Do you consider your own theorization of normative power compatible with the direction of Macherey's musings? I ask this because you discover a reconfigured space of agency in power's inevitable failure to achieve its intention; indeed, performative iterability seems to guarantee this failure. Yet as I read it, what Macherey finds interesting in this 'biological model' is that power's 'original' purpose is always/already multiple, contrary, disseminated, undecidable. It can only fail to achieve its purpose if it has 'one' (repression). Does this style of approach sit well with the spirit of your own intervention, despite its differences, or do you see problems with this reading?

Butler: I have great respect for Macherey's work, although perhaps I would not draw as strong a distinction between Hegel and Spinoza as he has done. I am wondering whether there is, though, in what you describe a certain figure of the 'biological' that presumes that it is 'multiple, contrary, disseminated, undecidable'. I worry that this imputes a certain critical or utopian power to the biological, and that the history and science of biology is itself set aside in favour of a rather idealist construal. It is also within the sphere of biology to discover fixation, recurrence, monotony, negativity and fatality, so I am not sure which rendition of the biological is at stake here or how one would adjudicate these differences.

I suppose that I am a Spinozist in some regards, although recently I wrote a piece arguing that Spinoza's inability to understand suicide as something self-induced shows us how thoroughly he has excised negativity from his notion of the conatus. Although it may be true that humans seek to persist in their own being, it is also true that sometimes they do not. And to follow your reasoning, it must be, as it were, biologically possible for humans to commit suicide. How do we understand this possibility of self-negation as constitutively human, and does it mean perhaps revisiting the labour of the negative in Hegel or the centrality of the death drive to the later Freud?

Kirby: It's interesting that you mention suicide here because it's one of the foundational questions in the history of sociology that returns us to the problematic of agency, causality, and the whole puzzle of the self and the social. Durkheim asks how such a very personal decision, whose reasons are felt as entirely individual, could *anticipate* larger social forces that articulate with gender, class and ethnicity differences, markers of age, place of residence and so on. And when you actually look at population statistics it's quite extraordinary to see that suicide rates form these legible and predictable signatures of pain in different subject formations, with definite temporal rhythms through the months of the year, and year after year, unless there is radical social change or intervention. I think Durkheim evokes a sense of organic cause here – and yet the organism *is* sociality, so none of us are displaced from be-ing that cause, intervening and reconfiguring its forms of animation. Perhaps this resonates with your criticism of Spinoza, inasmuch as suicide is never, at least straightfor-wardly, self-induced in Durkheim's reading. But is this about excising negativity, or acknowledging how a society, in myriad and incalculable ways, deems certain individual expressions of it*self*, its life, expendable, insufferable? Couldn't this way of thinking the corporate body resonate with your own work on abjection? If you could elaborate your work on Spinoza here that would be really helpful.

Butler: Let me say first that I agree that Durkheim asks us to begin by considering the social organization of life that brings suicide into being as a possibility. But what he cannot give us is the particular mechanics of subject formation that allow us to see how a certain subject turns to suicide and another not. In this way, for Durkheim, it is the social organization that commits the suicide, as it were, even as the suicide 'negates' that particular social world. In Spinoza, the 'cause' of suicide is always external, though not to be found in a particular social organization of life. You may remember in the *Ethics*, Spinoza remarks that no one commits suicide 'out of the necessity of his own nature' and suggests that suicidal desires can only be 'compelled by external causes' (Scholium to Proposition 20). Spinoza then distinguishes between forms of pleasure that diminish the desire to live and those that augment that desire. This suggests that we can understand forms of dying away, of the attrition of life, as modulations of pleasure and passion more generally. Emotions signify a certain human bondage, and this becomes most emphatically the case in passivity and servitude which, for him, undermine the more active possibility of persisting in desire and, hence, in the desire to live.

That said, however, Spinoza disputes that the desire no longer to exist can actually be derived from human desire, something he has already and consistently defined as the desire to persist in one's own being. When he imagines how suicide might be conducted, he writes, 'someone may kill himself if he is compelled by another, who twists the right hand which happens to be holding a sword'. He also cites the example from Seneca in which a suicide is coerced by a tyrant as a form of obligated political action. The third conjecture he offers is enigmatic since it promises an analysis it does not pursue. I try to pursue this to some degree in a recent paper. At one point, Spinoza remarks that a man may commit suicide 'because hidden external causes (*causae latentes externae*) so dispose his imagination and affect his body that it takes on (or contracts) another nature'. Here Spinoza acknowledges that the self can take its own life, but that the self *has acquired an external form* or, rather, an external cause has made its way into the structure of the self, lodged itself there and taken up residence as a permanently external 'cause' in the midst of the self. This internalized externality is thus responsible for any suicide. And in this way, Spinoza can continue to argue that a person takes his own life only by virtue of external causes, but not by any tendency internal to human desire itself, bound to life as it ostensibly is.

In a move that clearly prefigures psychoanalysis, Spinoza maintains that this external cause that houses itself in the self is something for which we cannot have an 'idea' and is, thus, an unconscious sort of operation. The 'I' is said to have taken on or contracted this externality, and so it has absorbed it through some means for which it has no representation, and *can have* no representation. Indeed, the 'I' becomes something other to itself in taking in this externality: it becomes, quite frankly, other to itself; and it is from this otherness, itself obdurate and obscure, that it can and does sometimes take its own life.

At this point it may be that Spinoza has himself admitted something into his theory that threatens the consistency of his account of desire, and that he has momentarily assumed the form of some other conception of desire, one which would orient it against life itself. And though I think here we can see a certain prefiguration of the death drive, one that is invoked for a moment in the commentary on the proposition only to be disposed of quite quickly, I would suggest that there are ways to see Spinoza's unsettled relation to a psychoanalysis he could have never anticipated. There is already, apart from the introduction of this hidden external cause in the life of desire, a way that externality works upon desire that modulates its relation to life itself.

Kirby: Throughout *Precarious Life* and several of your more recent essays, there is a real sense that a more capacious understanding of the human is urgently needed. In regard to this, and perhaps because so much of your work is a self-conscious engagement with Hegel, I'm reminded of your comment on Hyppolite's reading of the *Phenomenology* (contrasted against Kojève's), where you say 'Hyppolite does not ask after the being of "man," but after the being of "life." ' Of course, he does ask after 'man', but your point is that he can't begin his question if he thinks he already knows what it is to be a man, to be human.

How might this larger enframing of the question provide us with a different set of ethical and political considerations, a different way of understanding responsiveness to suffering, responsibility for suffering?

Butler: This is an excellent question, and I am not altogether sure I am prepared to answer it well at this moment. But I'll take it as a challenge to consider more carefully. One problem with using the framework of humanization and dehumanization is that it leaves the question of the animal to the side, and it tends to effect that separation of humans from other sentient beings that contributes to an anthropocentrism of a worrisome kind. So I suppose it is necessary to think more carefully about what we are trying to foreground when we claim, for instance, that torture is dehumanizing. At such moments, we call attention to the precariousness of life and the ethical demands that arise from that precariousness. The problem is not that a certain norm of the human has been abrogated, since the norms governing the recognizability of some humans over others as human is part of the problem. Rather, it is the failure to shelter and to regard the precariousness of life, that is, the susceptibility of a body to injury and violent death. At the same time, though, I would say that one needs to conduct a critique of the norm of the human in order to expose the way, for instance, human rights claims can be made on behalf of prisoners outside the US, but not within the US, and that certain populations deprived of juridical nation-state status are, it seems, precluded from eligibility for a human rights claim. In such cases, one has to remobilize the 'human' in order to create it anew, to give it, through performative force, a life where it has not had one before.

So I suppose that there are two projects at work here: the first is to consider the precariousness of life and the demands it makes upon us to safeguard bodies against destitution and destruction; the second is to conduct a critique of the 'human' as a norm, and to do this through asserting the human in those frameworks where it has had no 'right' to exist. Of course, one does the latter precisely in order to be more fully enabled to safeguard bodies against destitution and destruction. So perhaps the 'human' must be mobilized for the purposes of sheltering precarious life, but that 'life' takes us beyond the purview of the human to a broader problem of the vulnerability and exposure of sentient beings.

Kirby: At the time of this interview, your most recent works are *Undoing Gender* and *Precarious Life*. Could you talk about your forthcoming work, those publications that are already in the pipeline? And could you do a little crystal gazing and tell us what you see in your future research directions. What can we look forward to?

Butler: I've actually just published a book called *Giving an Account of Oneself* with Fordham University Press. I tried there to answer the question of whether a subject who is non-unitary and partially opaque to itself can nevertheless take responsibility and give an account of its actions. In a way, it's a foray into moral theory, but it also insists that efforts to give an account of the self demand that we take account as well of the social and discursive conditions of one's own emergence. This means that self-narration is linked with social theory. It also means that responsibility involves social critique. I try to take up Adorno's question of what it is to live a good life within a bad life, and I follow this up with some discussions of Foucault, some psycho-analytic thinkers, especially Laplanche, Levinas, and a bit of Kafka. My sense is that certain moral dispositions like humility and forgiveness are actually based on the recognition that we are all to some degree opaque about why we do what we do and that our narratives fail to be seamless and unified in the way that some imagine a story of a life can be.

In my recent work, I have sought to understand what it is to give an account of oneself when one is not fully transparent to oneself, when one cannot always relate one's life in narrative form, and when the social and linguistic conditions of one's own existence are not always fully understood or available to a narrative account. Although I am certainly not against narrative in any strong sense – I think, frankly, we all need to be able to give some accounts of ourselves in order to live and survive – I think it is equally implausible though to demand that a life always conform to the criterion of a story. Of course, one gives an account of oneself to someone, and so it seems to be that the account is not only an account that I give of myself and to myself.

It is an effort to make oneself known, and it requires a structure of address as well as an other for whom my account might matter in some way. Indeed, others sometimes ask us to give an account of why we have done what we have done, and we seek to make ourselves understood, if we do, in order to sustain the relationship between oneself and the other. Indeed, giving an account is rarely a solitary act, since even if I sought to give an account only to myself, I would have to act as both speaker and audience to the story at issue. The account still requires its recipient, and there is still a question of whether I can offer the kind of account that might satisfy the narrative requirements of a full and seamless story. Let's assume that not only in the cases of extreme trauma that beset an author like Primo Levi, but in the course of life itself, there are gaps or fissures in the accounts that we give, and that we have no account to give of why that part of life cannot be recalled or given in narrative form. This becomes especially acute when we ask others, or ourselves, to give an account of themselves in order precisely to hold them accountable for their actions, in an effort to locate or assign responsibility of a set of actions that led to injurious consequences. In such cases, we depend upon the capacity of another to give an account in order to determine responsibility, and when and where that capacity breaks down, we turn to other kinds of evidence to determine the agency of the action at issue. In courts of law, such a juridical notion of responsibility is operative, and clearly it must be. But are we right to import such a model of responsibility into non-juridical domains of human relationality? Could it be that there are other ethical values that are lost when the juridical notion of accountability becomes equated with our understanding of responsibility more generally?

I ask this question because it would seem that if traumatic events make giving an account difficult or impossible, some compassion toward this inability to narrate the issue of agency is important to maintain. Moreover, the 'I' who would make itself into the inaugural moment of a sequence of acts is one who places itself at the centre of the action in question, when sometimes a series of circumstances and actors are acting upon the scene at once, all of which are acted on by other circumstances and actors, the history of which cannot be fully known or narrated at the time, if ever. Indeed, it would seem to me that there is some humility to be valued in recognizing that one's actions are not always completely and utterly originating with the 'I' that one is, and that, correspondingly, there is some forgiveness to offer to others and perhaps also to oneself when and if it becomes clear that giving a full account of oneself is impossible.

Kirby: To return to an earlier point, you were talking about the directions in your future work?

Butler: I've also begun a longer project on Jewish philosophy, concentrating on those thinkers who have formulated a critique of state violence both prior to the establishment of Israel in 1948 and since. I've worked extensively on Benjamin's critique of violence, and am interested as well in the work of Hermann Cohen and Franz Rosenzweig, both of whom thought a 'state' and 'land' for the Jews was not a good idea. Of course, that position becomes harder to maintain after the Shoah, but I am interested in a diasporic conception of Judaism and whether it can and has furnished some important tools for being able to speak one's criticism of Israel without vacating Jewishness itself. I'm reading as well Martin Buber's political writings and, most recently, Primo Levi, whose political views against state violence seem to follow from his analysis of the concentration camps. I believe this actually links him to some of Edward Said's late work, and I'm interested in thinking through binationalism as a way of moving beyond identitarian politics.

In Said's *Freud and the Non-European*, he argues that Judaism has a diasporic beginning and that this continues to inform strains of Judaism that are not centred on nationalism or the nation-state. He refers there to Moses as a 'non-European' founder of Judaism, suggesting that there is in Moses a complex identity, Jewish and Egyptian, and that the Egyptian participates in what is non-Jewish. This participation in life with the non-Jew is, I think, the basis of a diasporic conception of Judaism, one that is committed to forms of living together with the non-Jew as part of its constitutive ethicality. He makes a further point that I appreciate, which is that there are divergent legacies of displacement that characterize Palestinians and Jews alike, and that, ideally, these histories could produce a binational polity that would be founded on a certain notion of sanctuary for refugees, displaced persons, those in need of shelter. He quite beautifully lays out this impossible ideal of binationalism, and in my view it would involve not 'two' nationalisms, but a joint effort to live to the side of a nationalist ethos.

Although Said clearly had his problems with post-structuralism, it is interesting to me that in this late work he would prize those forms of sociality that undo the unitary nature of the political subject. He understood that only through such an undoing could cohabitation be realized. It is a position that moves beyond identitarianism and pluralism alike.

Kirby: It seems to me that you move very well beyond identitiarian philosophies and theories too, from German speculative philosophy, to the French material, Jewish philosophy, and then there's an inter-weaving with literature and popular culture in your work as well. Are there difficulties in doing this?

Butler: Frankly, there are no difficulties for me in doing this, but I gather that there are readers who have some problems with the movements among such texts. I think that I entered the question of desire and recognition in Hegel, for instance, from a problem that emerged for me as a queer young person who preferred sitting in the basement of my parents' home reading Spinoza to other forms of available sociality. Probably there were translations at work for me in reading philosophy, ones that I have not always been able to uncover or explain to my readers. At other times, I have been engaged by films (*Boys Don't Cry*) or contemporary events (the riots in Los Angeles surrounding the Rodney King events), or contemporary political debates (censorship, Zionism, gay marriage). I suppose that I bring a certain philosophical perspective on my thinking about these issues. But it is always an issue that prompts my thinking, some way that my world is organized that leaves me vexed and in need of clarification. I think it is probably fair to say that I am one of those people who is always trying to figure out how to live, and so my reference points are both particular and social and political, and also more generally philosophical. The latter emerges from the question of how to live. I appreciated that in his final interview, Derrida remarks that he has never learned how to live, that this form of knowledge has eluded him his whole life. I laughed with appreciation at this final remark. He remains within the Socratic problematic, trying to learn how best to live, but he despairs of any possible accumulation of knowledge on the matter. It is a fine joke, in a way, one that gives the rest of us a certain permission to live without quite knowing whether we are doing it right.

Notes

Chapter 1: Precarious Foundations – *Subjects of Desire: Hegelian Reflections in Twentieth-Century France*

1. The book is a revision of her doctoral thesis, *Recovery and Invention: The Projects of Desire in Hegel, Kojève, Hyppolite and Sartre*, Yale University, 1984.
2. In Kojève and Hyppolite Butler finds a sufficient difference of approach to explore the provocative energy in French Hegelianism. Both men translated and lectured on Hegel's work and published extensive commentaries on Hegel's *Phenomenology of Spirit*, and those who attended their classes were among the intellectual luminaries of their time. Scholars such as Maurice Merleau-Ponty, Georges Bataille, Jean Desanti and Jacques Lacan attended Kojève's lectures during 1933–39. And Michel Foucault, Louis Althusser, Jacques Derrida and Gilles Deleuze were among Hyppolite's students when he began teaching over a decade later.
3. For an excellent introduction to the internal workings of language, see Émile Benveniste, *Problems in General Linguistics* (1971).
4. Consistent with this point it is important to appreciate that Butler's interpretation of Hegel is an interested reading, one which looks to further certain implications and suggestive possibilities in his text while inevitably ignoring others. In a review essay of Michael S. Roth's *Knowing and History: Appropriations of Hegel in Twentieth-Century France*, Butler notes approvingly that Roth ignores the question of 'whether or not the French "got Hegel right,"' and concurs that 'that question is fundamentally unimportant for the consideration of the meaning of French Hegelianism … the verificationist impulse has no place here' (1990a, 249). Although the 'verificationist impulse' cannot be dismissed cavalierly, Butler's reasons for rejecting it prove just as pertinent to a commentary such as this one.

5. The maze of implication continues, however, for the identity of human species-being, when read through the question of species-being more generally, will again dissolve and become a much more problematic 'thing' which incorporates the informational structures of other life forms.

6. A significant body of feminist research has shown that the history of philosophy is consistent in masculinizing reason and feminizing the corporeal as both dangerous and extraneous to reason. See, for example, Irigaray (1985a), Moller Okin (1979), Lloyd (1993).

7. Hegel's criticisms of Descartes' cogito, a divided unity of mind and body, is consistent with this: '[w]ith Descartes corporeality and the thinking "I" are altogether independent Beings; this independence of the two extremes is done away with in Spinozism by their becoming moments of the one absolute being' (Hegel cited in Butler 1987a, 11–12). In Spinoza's monism Hegel recognized a valuable precursor to his own dialectic of identity.

8. The difference between Kojève's and Hyppolite's reading of the *Phenomenology* rehearses this important question. Butler notes that for Kojève, 'desire only becomes truly human, fully transformative, when it takes on a non-natural object, namely, another human consciousness' (1987a, 68). For Kojève, the difference between consciousness (human being) and the world is an ontological difference that can't be overcome. 'In Kojève's view, the sensuous aspect of human identity is precisely what calls for transcendence.' Only through this separation can desire operate as 'a unilateral action upon the world in which consciousness instates itself as the generator of historical reality' (Butler 1987a, 69). Hyppolite counters the restrictive anthropocentrism of this reading and its buoyant progression towards enlightenment. As Butler notes, 'Hyppolite does not ask after the being of "man," but after the being of "life"; through this return to Life, the imparting and dissolution of shape, Hyppolite finds the absolute as both dynamic and thoroughly monistic' (Butler 1987a, 82).

Chapter 2: Gender, Sexuality, Performance –
Gender Trouble: Feminism and the Subversion of Identity

1. This position is exemplified in Adrienne Rich's notion of the 'lesbian continuum' (1983).

2. See Luce Irigaray, *This Sex Which Is Not One* (1985b).

3. The following interview, an assessment of Irigaray's past significance and contemporary relevance, represents two very different ap-

proaches. Grosz and Cheah contend that Irigaray's work has a more global political pertinence than Butler and Cornell will concede. Indeed, Butler and Cornell argue that the need to attribute such universal relevance is politically misguided. See Butler *et al.* (1998b).

4. See, especially, Claude Lévi-Strauss (1968; 1969).

5. In 'The Confession of the Flesh' Foucault responds to a question from Jacques-Alain Miller about the difference between the discursive and non-discursive. When pressed, Foucault underlines that as his real concern isn't 'a linguistic one', and as institutional ('non-discursive') forces, although not utterances, are nevertheless socially learned, the distinction is largely irrelevant to him (1980b, 198).

Chapter 3: Gender, Sexuality, Performance –
Bodies that Matter: On the Discursive Limits of "Sex"

1. See, for example, D. B. Morris, *The Culture of Pain* (1991).

2. The reference to 'Bisexuality' in Laplanche and Pontalis, *The Language of Psychoanalysis* (1973), is helpful here.

3. The importance of the term 'consubstantial' will reappear in reference to the Saussurean sign's paradoxical identity – an 'entity' whose invariance is made possible by a system of referral that is pure variation.

Chapter 4: Language, Power, Performativity –
Bodies that Matter: On the Discursive Limits of "Sex"

1. Although Butler is aware of the following work, describing it as 'a reading of Lacan which argues that prohibition or, more precisely, the bar is foundational (1993a, 268), she does not acknowledge its critical implications for her own position. See Jean-Luc Nancy and Philippe Lacoue-Labarthe, *The Title of the Letter: A Reading of Lacan* (1992). For an analysis of the Saussurean sign that also contests Butler's interpretation, see Jacques Derrida *Of Grammatology* (1984), and Vicki Kirby *Telling Flesh* (1997).

2. An excellent example of how arguments from biology and even physics might actually further Butler's aims rather than hinder them can be seen in the work of biosemiotician Jesper Hoffmeyer, who argues that the biosphere is a semiosphere. See his *Signs of Meaning in the Universe* (1996). Similarly, Karen Barad, a feminist and physicist of quantum mechanics, acknowledges the puzzling animation of

matter and the inseparability of scientific models and their objects. See *Meeting the Universe Halfway* (forthcoming); and also the important work of Elizabeth A. Wilson, *Psychosomatic: Feminism and the Neurological Body* (2004). Such contributions to the *question* of matter are compatible with Butler's political project, even though they radically extend its terms.

3. For another perspective on the reasons why Butler's uncritical commitment to the sign's identity effectively sabotages her project, see Pheng Cheah (1996).

Chapter 5: Language, Power, Performativity –
Excitable Speech: A Politics of the Performative

1. An expression commonly attributed to Jacques Derrida, it was actually used by Althusser to capture the inadequacy of causal explanations that rely on linear notions of time.

2. And yet it seems that this all-encompassing ideological enclosure is somewhat qualified for the theorist. Althusser's personal 'mission' was to find something exceptional in science that would provide an objective platform for a scientific understanding of ideology.

3. Butler dilates on this reading in Butler and Bell (1999c, 169).

4. Of immediate interest here is MacKinnon (1993), Matsuda *et al.* (1993) and Langton (1993).

5. We should note in passing that MacKinnon's position is not based on an assumption that reality is an enfolded nest of illusional replacements, but, as Butler describes it, her position rests on a 'more original ... normative or utopian' reality whose authority is not in question (Butler 1997b, 66).

6. For a detailed explication of this point, see, especially, Foucault (1979). See also Anna Bennett's doctoral thesis on Foucault (2001).

7. Although Butler certainly acknowledges this point (1997b, 23) she is unable to maintain its implications in her argument's overall direction.

8. Indeed, Butler seems reluctant fully to open the question of pornography to an erotics of pleasure/pain that might not fit the political functionalism of those forms that meet her approval: '*graphic self-representation*, as in Mapplethorpe's photography; *explicit self-declaration*, such as that which takes place in the practice of coming out; and *explicit sexual education*, as in AIDS education (1997b, 22).

Chapter 6: Identity and Politics – *The Psychic Life of Power: Theories of Subjection. Undoing Gender*

1. See, for example, Foucault (1979) and (1980a).
2. Of course, if we concede that power's identity is problematic from the start, then there is no necessary reason to interpret the panopticon as an apparatus of domination and control. If there is no *one* in the tower, then the apparatus is as much a *dispositif* of creative reflection, re-cognition and invention as it is one of surveillance and compliance. Even in prisons, prisoners invent and even flaunt myriad forms of encryption, secret languages that can 'in-habit' the very norms they flout.
3. See Butler's 'Foucault and the Paradox of Bodily Inscriptions' (1989a).
4. In this regard, we might note the fascinating citation in Mikkel Borch-Jacobsen to Etienne de la Boétie:

> He who thus domineers over you has only two eyes, only two hands, only one body, no more than is possessed by the least man among the infinite numbers dwelling in your cities; he has indeed nothing more than the power that you confer upon him to destroy you. Where has he acquired enough eyes to spy upon you, if you do not provide them yourselves? How can he have so many arms to beat you with, if he does not borrow them from you? The feet that trample down your cities, where does he get them if they are not your own? How does he have any power over you except through you? (1999, 153)

Chapter 7: Butler on Others – Others on Butler

1. At the time of writing, a conservative Australian government has 'banded' disciplines in terms of weighted values that justify the distribution of government monies. Needless to say, philosophy, literature and history are at the bottom.
2. Butler is infamous for receiving first prize in the fourth Bad Writing Contest, sponsored by the conservative academic journal *Philosophy and Literature*. See her response (1999b).
3. For a good reference base of reviews and criticisms of Butler's work to the end of 2001, see E. Yeghiayan, http://sun3.lib.uci.edu/indiv/scctr/Wellek/butler/html.
4. In 'Merely Cultural' (1997c), Butler makes reference to Fraser's *Justice Interruptus* (1997a). Fraser responds in 'Heterosexism, Misrecognition and Capitalism: A Response to Judith Butler' (1997).

Bibliography

Butler titles

(1982), 'The German question', translation of Herbert Ammon and Peter Brandt's 'Die Deutsche Frage', *Telos*, 51, 32–45.

(1982), 'Review of Joseph Fell's "Heidegger and Sartre: An essay on being and place"', *Philosophical Review*, 91 (4), 641–5.

(1982), 'Seven taboos and a perspective', translation of Rudolph Bahro and Michael Vester's 'Sieben Tabus und eine Perspektive', *Telos*, 51, 45–52.

(1984), 'Recovery and invention: The projects of desire in Hegel, Kojève, Hyppolite and Sartre', PhD dissertation, Yale University.

(1985), *'Geist ist Zeit*: French interpretations of Hegel's Absolute', *Berkshire Review*, 20, 66–80.

(1986), 'Desire and recognition in Sartre's *Saint Genet* and *The Family Idiot*, Vol. 1', *International Philosophical Quarterly*, 26 (4), 359–74.

(1986), 'Sex and gender in Simone de Beauvoir's *Second Sex*', *Yale French Studies*, 72, 35–49.

(1986), 'Variations on sex and gender: Beauvoir, Wittig, and Foucault', *Praxis International*, 5, 505–16.

(1987a), *Subjects of Desire: Hegelian Reflections in Twentieth-Century France* (New York: Columbia University Press).

(1987), 'Gender, the family and history', review of Linda Nicholson's *Gender and History: The Limits of Social Theory in the Age of the Family*, *Praxis International*, 7 (1), 125–30.

(1987), 'Variations on sex and gender: Beauvoir, Wittig, and Foucault', in S. Benhabib and D. Cornell (eds), *Feminism as Critique: Essays on the Politics of Gender in Late-Capitalist Societies* (Cambridge, UK: Polity Press, 128–42).

(1988), 'Performative acts and gender constitution: An essay in phenomenology and feminist theory', *Theatre Journal*, 49 (1), 519–31.

(1988), Review of Edith Wyschogrod's *Spirit in Ashes: Hegel, Heidegger, and Man-Made Mass Death*, History and Theory, 27 (1), 60–70.

(1988), Review of Gilles Deleuze and Claire Parnet's *Dialogues*, Canadian Philosophical Reviews, 8 (5), 163–6.

(1989a), 'Foucault and the paradox of bodily inscriptions', *Journal of Philosophy*, 86 (11), 601–7.

(1989), 'The body politics of Julia Kristeva', *Hypatia: Journal of Feminist Philosophy*, 3 (3), 104–18.

(1989), 'Gendering the body: Beauvoir's philosophical contribution', in A. Garry and M. Pearsall (eds), *Women, Knowledge, and Reality: Explorations in Feminist Philosophy* (Boston: Unwin Hyman), 253–62.

(1989), 'Response to Joseph Flay's "Hegel, Derrida and Bataille's Laughter"', in W. Desmond (ed.), *Hegel and His Critics: Philosophy in the Aftermath of Hegel* (Albany, NY: SUNY Press), 174–8.

(1989), Review of A. Nye's *Feminist Theory and the Philosophies of Man* Canadian Philosophical Reviews, 9 (8), 326–8.

(1989), Review of C. Weedon's *Feminist Practice and Post-Structuralist Theory*, Ethics, 99 (3), 668–9.

(1989), 'Sexual ideology and phenomenological description: A feminist critique of Merleau-Ponty's *Phenomenology of Perception*', in J. Allen and M. Young (eds), *The Thinking Muse: Feminism and Modern French Philosophy* (Bloomington and Indianapolis: Indiana University Press), 85–100.

(1990a), Review of M. S. Roth's *Knowing and History: Appropriations of Hegel in Twentieth-Century France*, History and Theory, 29 (2), 248–58.

(1990b), *Gender Trouble: Feminism and the Subversion of Identity* (New York and London: Routledge).

(1990), 'Comments on Bernasconi, Cornell, Weber: Deconstruction and the possibility of justice', *Cardozo Law Review*, 11 (5–6), 1715–18.

(1990), 'The force of fantasy: Feminism, Mapplethorpe, and discursive excess', *differences: A Journal of Feminist Cultural Studies*, 2 (2), 105–25.

(1990), 'Gender trouble, feminist theory, and psychoanalytic discourse', in L. J. Nicholson (ed.), *Feminism/Postmodernism* (New York: Routledge), 324–40.

(1990), 'Jean-Paul Sartre (1905–1980)', in G. Stade (ed.), *European Writers: The Twentieth Century*, Vol. 12 (New York: Scribner), 2589–614.

(1990), 'Lana's "Imitation": Melodramatic repetition and the gender performative', *Genders*, 9, 1–18.

(1990), 'Performative acts and gender constitution: An essay in phenomenology and feminist theory', in S. Case (ed.), *Performing*

Feminisms: Feminist Critical Theory and Theatre (Baltimore, MD: Johns Hopkins University Press), 270–82.

(1990), 'The pleasures of repetition', in R. A. Glick and S. Bone (eds), *Pleasure Beyond the Pleasure Principle* (New Haven, CT and London: Yale University Press), 259–75.

(1990), Review of P. Dews' *The Logics of Disintegration: Poststructuralist Thought and the Claims of Critical Theory*, *International Studies in Philosophy*, 22 (3), 79–82.

(1991), 'On Catherine MacKinnon's *Towards a Feminist Theory of State*, and Carole Pateman's *The Disorder of Women*', *Transition: An International Review*, 53, 86–95.

(1991), 'Contingent foundations: Feminism and the question of "postmodernism"', *Praxis International*, 11 (2), 150–65.

(1991), 'Imitation and gender insubordination' in D. Fuss (ed.), *Inside/Out: Lesbian Theories, Gay Theories* (New York: Routledge), 13–31.

(1991), 'A note on performative acts of violence', *Cardozo Law Review*, 13 (4), 1303–4.

(1991), 'The nothing that is: Wallace Stevens' Hegelian affinities', in B. Cowan and J. G. Kronick (eds), *Theorizing American Literature: Hegel, the Sign, and History* (Baton Rouge and London: Louisiana State University Press), 269–87.

(1991), 'Response to Teri Shearer's review of *Gender Trouble: Feminism and the Subversion of Identity*', *The Journal of Social Epistemology*, 5 (4), 345–8.

and Kotz, L. (1992a), 'The body you want: An interview with Judith Butler', *Artforum*, 31 (3), 82–9.

(1992), 'On Achille Mbembe's "The banality of power and the aesthetics of vulgarity in the postcolony"', *Public Culture*, 4 (2), 1–30.

(1992), 'The body politics of Julia Kristeva', in N. Fraser and S. L. Bartky (eds), *Revaluing French Feminism: Critical Essays on Difference, Agency, and Culture* (Bloomington and Indianapolis: Indiana University Press), 162–76.

(1992), 'Contingent foundations: Feminism and the question of "postmodernism"', in J. Butler and J. W. Scott (eds), *Feminists Theorize the Political* (New York and London: Routledge), 3–21.

(1992), 'Gender', in E. Wright, D. Chisholm, J. F. MacCannell and M. Whitford (eds), *Feminism and Psychoanalysis: A Critical Dictionary* (Oxford and Cambridge: Blackwell), 140–5.

(1992), 'The lesbian phallus and the morphological imaginary', *differences: A Journal of Feminist Cultural Studies*, 4 (1), 133–71.

(1992), 'Mmembe's extravagant power', *Public Culture: Bulletin of the Society for Transnational Cultural Studies*, 5 (1), 67–74.

(1992), 'Response to Bordo's "Feminist scepticism and the 'maleness' of philosophy"', *Hypatia: A Journal of Feminist Philosophy*, 7 (3), 162–5.

(1992), 'Sexual inversions: Rereading the end of Foucault's *History of Sexuality, Vol. I*, in D. C. Stanton (ed.), *Discourses of Sexuality: From Aristotle to AIDS* (Ann Arbor: University of Michigan Press), 344–61.

and Aronowitz, S., Bhabha, H., Laclau, E., Mouffe, C., Scott, J. and West. C. (1992), 'Discussion', *October*, 61, 108–20.

and MacGrogan, M. (1992), 'Editor's Introduction', in J. Butler and M. MacGrogan (eds), *Linda Singer's Erotic Welfare: Sexual Theory and Politics in the Age of Epidemic* (New York and London: Routledge), 1–15.

and Nash, M. (1992), Interview, 'Judith Butler: Singing the body', *Bookpress*, 2 (2), 5–12.

and Scott, J. W. (1992), 'Introduction', in J. Butler and J. W. Scott (eds), *Feminists Theorize the Political* (New York and London: Routledge), xiii–xvii.

(1993a), *Bodies that Matter: On the Discursive Limits of "Sex"* (New York and London: Routledge).

(1993), 'The body politics of Julia Kristeva', in K. Oliver (ed.), *Ethics, Politics, and Difference in Julia Kristeva's Writings: A Collection of Essays* (New York and London: Routledge), 164–78.

(1993), 'Critically queer', *GLQ – A Journal of Lesbian and Gay Studies*, 1 (1), 17–32.

(1993), 'Decamping', Letter to the Editor, *Lingua Franca*, 4 (1), 5.

(1993), 'Endangered/endangering: Schematic racism and white paranoia', in R. Gooding-Williams (ed.), *Reading Rodney King/Reading Urban Uprising* (New York and London: Routledge), 15–22.

(1993), 'Imitation and gender insubordination', in H. Abelove, M. A. Barale and D. M. Halperin (eds), *The Lesbian and Gay Studies Reader* (New York and London: Routledge), 307–20.

(1993), 'Interview', *Neid*, 1 (1), 8–9.

(1993), 'Kierkegaard's speculative despair', in R. C. Solomon and K. M. Higgins (eds), *German Idealism* (London and New York: Routledge), 363–95.

(1993), 'Poststructuralism and postmarxism', *Diacritics*, 23 (4), 3–11.

(1993), 'Response to Sarah Kofman', *Compar(a)ison: An International Journal of Comparative Literature*, 1 (1), 27–32.

(1993), 'A sceptical feminist postscript to the postmodern', in B. Readings and B. Schaber (eds), *Postmodernism Across the Ages: Essays for a Postmodernity that Wasn't Born Yesterday* (Syracuse, NY: Syracuse University Press), 233–7.

(1993), 'Sexual inversions', in J. Caputo and M. Yount (eds), *Foucault and the Critique of Institutions* (University Park: Pennsylvania State University Press), 81–98.

and Greaney, P. and Wittman, E. O. (1993), 'An interview with Judith Butler', *Yale Literary Magazine*, 4 (2), 46.

(1994), 'Against proper objects', *differences: A Journal of Feminist Cultural Studies*, 6 (2–3), 1–27.

(1994), 'Bodies that matter', in C. Burke, N. Schor and M. Whitford (eds), *Engaging with Irigaray: Feminist Philosophy and Modern European Thought* (New York: Columbia University Press), 141–73.

(1994), 'Contingent foundations: Feminism and the question of "postmodernism"', in S. Seidman (ed.), *The Postmodern Turn: New Perspectives on Social Theory* (Cambridge and New York: Cambridge University Press), 153–70.

(1994), 'Critical exchanges: The symbolic and questions of gender', in H. J. Silverman (ed.), *Continental Philosophy*, (5) (New York and London: Routledge), 134–49.

(1994), 'Kantians in every culture?', *Boston Review*, 19 (5), 18.

(1994), 'Sexual traffic', an interview with Gayle Rubin, *differences: A Journal of Feminist Cultural Studies*, 6 (2–3), 62–99.

with Braidotti, R. (1994), Interview, 'Feminism by any other name', *differences: A Journal of Feminist Cultural Studies*, 6 (2–3), 27–61.

with Osborne, P. and Segal, L. (1994), Interview, 'Gender as performance', *Radical Philosophy*, 67, 32–9.

and Martin. B. (eds), (1994), Editor's Introduction – 'Cross-identifications', *Diacritics*, 24 (2–3), 3.

and Benhabib, S., Cornell, D. and Fraser, N. (1995a), *Feminist Contentions: A Philosophical Exchange* (New York: Routledge).

(1995), 'Burning acts: Injurious speech', in A. Haverkamp (ed.), *Deconstruction is/in America: A New Sense of the Political* (New York: New York University Press), 149–80.

(1995), 'Burning Acts – Injurious speech', in A. Parker and E. Kosofsky Sedgwick (eds), *Performativity and Performance* (New York and London: Routledge), 197–227.

(1995), 'Collected and fractured: Response to *Identities*', in K. A. Appiah and H. L. Gates, Jr (eds), *Identities* (Chicago and London: University of Chicago Press), 439–47.

(1995), 'Conscience doth make subjects of us all', *Yale French Studies*, 88, 6–26.

(1995), 'Contingent foundations: Feminism and the question of "postmodernism"', in C. Caruth and D. Esch (eds), *Critical Encounters: Reference and Responsibility in Deconstructive Writing* (New Brunswick, NJ: Rutgers University Press, 213–32.

(1995), 'Desire', in F. Lentricchia and T. McLaughlin (eds), *Critical Terms for Literary Study*, 2nd edition (Chicago and London: University of Chicago Press), 369–86.

(1995), 'Keeping it moving: "Melancholy gender – refused identification"', *Psychoanalytic Dialogues*, 5 (2), 189–93.

(1995), 'Melancholy gender/refused identification', in M. Berger, B. Wallis and S. Watson (eds), *Constructing Masculinity* (New York and London: Routledge), 21–36.

(1995), 'Response to Régis Debray on *Transmitting Symbols*, and Manfred Frank on *Mental Intimacy and Epistemic Self-Ascription*', *Common Knowledge*, 4 (2), 70–3.

(1995), 'Slaying the messenger', Letter to the Editor, *New York Times*, June 8, A18 (national edition), A28 (local edition).

(1995), 'Stubborn attachment, bodily subjection: Rereading Hegel on the unhappy consciousness', in T. Rajan and D. L. Clark (eds), *Intersections: Nineteenth-Century Philosophy and Contemporary Theory* (Albany, NY: SUNY Press), 173–96.

(1995), 'Subjection, resistance, resignification: Between Freud and Foucault', in J. Rajchman (ed.), *The Identity in Question* (New York and London: Routledge), 229–49.

(1995), 'Thresholds of melancholy', in S. G. Crowell (ed.), *The Prism of the Self: Philosophical Essays in Honor of Maurice Natanson* (Dordrecht, Holland and Boston: Kluwer), 3–12.

(1995), 'On William J. Bennett and C. C. DeLores Tucker's op-ed "Lyrics from the Gutter"', *New York Times*, June 2, A29 (local edition).

(1996), 'An affirmative view', *Representations*, 55, 74–83.

(1996), 'Gender trouble: Feminism and the subject', in M. Eagleton (ed.), *Feminist Literary Theory: A Reader*, 2nd edition (Oxford, UK and Cambridge, MA: Blackwell), 367–73.

(1996), 'Imitation and gender insubordination', in A. Garry and M. Pearsall (eds), *Women, Knowledge, and Reality* (New York and London: Routledge), 371–87.

(1996), 'Sexual inversions', in S. J. Hekman (ed.), *Feminist Interpretations of Michel Foucault* (University Park: Pennsylvania State University Press), 59–75.

(1996), 'Status, conduct, word, and deed: A response to Janet Halley', *GLQ: A Journal of Lesbian and Gay Studies*, 3 (2–3), 253–9.

(1996), 'Universality in culture', in J. Cohen (ed.), *For Love of Country: Debating the Limits of Patriotism: Martha C. Nussbaum with Respondents* (Boston, MA: Beacon Press), 45–52.

(1996), 'Variations on sex and gender: Beauvoir, Wittig and Foucault', in P. Rice and P. Waugh (eds), *Modern Literary Theory: A Reader*, 3rd edition (London and New York: Arnold), 145–59.

with Osborne, P. (1996), Interview, in P. Osborne (ed.), *A Critical Sense: Interviews with Intellectuals* (London and New York: Routledge).

(1997a), *The Psychic Life of Power: Theories of Subjection* (Stanford, CA: Stanford University Press).

(1997b), *Excitable Speech: A Politics of the Performative* (New York and London: Routledge).

(1997c), 'Merely cultural', *Social Text*, 52–3, 265–77.

(1997), 'Excerpt from "Introduction" to *Bodies that Matter*', in R. N. Lancaster and M. di Leonardo (eds), *The Gender/Sexuality Reader: Culture, History, Political Economy* (New York and London: Routledge), 531–42.

(1997), 'Further reflections on conversations of our time', *Diacritics*, 27 (1), 13–15.

(1997), 'Gender is burning: Questions of appropriation and subversion', in A. McClintock, A. Mufti and E. Shohat (eds), *Dangerous Liaisons: Gender, Nation, and Postcolonial Perspectives* (Minneapolis: University of Minnesota Press), 381–95.

(1997), 'Imitation and gender subordination', in L. Nicholson (ed.), *The Second Wave: A Reader in Feminist Theory* (New York and London: Routledge, 300–15.

(1997), 'In Memoriam: Maurice Natanson (1924–1996)'. *Review of Metaphysics*, 50, (3), 739–740.

(1997), 'Performative acts and gender constitution: An essay in phenomenology and feminist theory', in K. Conboy, N. Medina and S. Stanbury (eds), *Writing on the Body: Female Embodiment and Feminist Theory* (New York: Columbia University Press), 401–17.

(1997), 'Queering, passing: Nella Larsen's *Passing*', in E. Abel, B. Christian and H. Moglen (eds), *Female Subjects in Black and White: Race, Psychoanalysis, Feminism* (Berkeley, CA: University of California Press), 266–84.

(1997), 'Response to Lynne Layton's "The doer behind the deed: Tensions and intersections between Butler's vision of performativity and relational psychoanalysis"', *Gender and Psychoanalysis*, 2 (4), 515–20.

(1997), 'Sovereign performatives in the contemporary scene of utterance', *Critical Inquiry*, 23 (2), 350–77.

(1997), 'Subjects of sex/gender/desire', in S. Kemp and J. Squires (eds), *Feminisms* (Oxford and New York: Oxford University Press), 278–85.

(1997), 'On transexuality: Excitable speech', an interview with K. More. *Radical Deviance: A Transgendered Politics*, 2, 134–43.

and Laclau, E. and Laddaga, R. (1997), 'The uses of equality', *Diacritics*, 27 (1), 3–12.

and McMillen, L. (1997), Interview, 'Judith Butler revels in the role of troublemaker', *Chronicle of Higher Education*, 43 (27), May 23, A14–A15.

and Worsely, K. (1997), Interview, *Times Higher Education Supplement*, 1 (280), May 16, 20.

Meijer, I. C. and Prins, B. (1998a), 'How bodies come to matter: An interview with Judith Butler', *Signs*, 23 (1), 275–86.

and Cornell, D., Cheah, P. and Grosz, E. (1998b), 'The future of sexual difference: An Interview with Judith Butler and Drucilla Cornell (with Pheny Gheah and Elizabeth Grosz)', *Diacritics*, 28 (1), 19–42.

(1998), 'Afterword', in S. R. Munt (ed.), *Butch/femme: Inside lesbian gender* (London: Cassell), 225–31.

(1998), 'Analysis to the core: Commentary on papers by James Hansell and Dianne Elise', *Psychoanalytic Dialogues*, 8 (3), 399–403.

(1998), 'Athletic genders: Hyperbolic instance and/or the overcoming of sexual binarism in the athlete's body', *Stanford Humanities Review*, 6 (2), 103–11.

(1998), 'Foreword', in M. Natanson, *The Erotic Bird: Phenomenology in Literature* (Princeton, NJ: Princeton University Press), ix–xvi.

1998), 'Left conservatism 2', *Theory and Event*, 2 (2), an online journal.

(1998), 'Merely cultural', *New Left Review*, 227, 33–44.

(1998), 'Moral sadism and doubting one's own love', in J. Phillips and L. Stonebridge (eds), *Reading Melanie Klein* (London and New York: Routledge), 179–89.

(1998), 'Response to Robert Gooding-Williams on "Multiculturalism and democracy"', *Constellations: An International Journal of Critical and Democratic Theory*, 5 (1), 42–7.

(1998), 'Ruled out: Vocabularies of the censor', in R. C. Post (ed.), *Censorship and Silencing: Practices of Cultural Regulation* (Los Angeles: Getty Research Institute for the History of Art and the Humanities), 247–59.

(1998), 'Sex and gender in Simone de Beauvoir's *Second Sex*', in E. Fallaize (ed.), *Simone de Beauvoir: A Critical Reader* (London and New York: Routledge), 30–42.

(1998), 'Troubling philosophy: An interview with Judith Butler', *Women's Philosophy Review*, 18, Spring, 7–21.

(1998), 'Where is Europe going?', *New Left Review*, 227, 33–4.

and Vaisman, D. (1998), 'Power and the name', Interview, *Meteorite*, 1 (1), 53–8.

(1999a), *Subjects of Desire: Hegelian Reflections in Twentieth-Century France*

(New York: Columbia University Press), reprint with a new introduction.

(1999b), 'A "bad writer" bites back', *New York Times*, March 20, A27.

and Bell, V. J. (1999c), Interview. 'On speech, race and melancholia', *Theory Culture & Society*, 16 (2), 163–74.

(1999), 'Contagious word: Paranoia and "homosexuality" in the military', in D. Batstone and E. Mendieta (eds), *The Good Citizen* (New York: Routledge), 133–58.

(1999), *Gender Trouble: Feminism and the Subversion of Identity*, 10th Anniversary Edition (New York: Routledge).

(1999), 'Headnote to Stanley Fish's "There's no such thing as free speech, and it's a good thing, too"', in H. Aram Veeser (ed.), *The Stanley Fish Reader* (Malden, MA and Oxford: Blackwell), 144–5.

(1999), 'Performativity's social magic', in R. Shusterman (ed.), *Bourdieu: A Critical Reader* (Oxford and Malden, MA: Blackwell), 113–29.

and Bell, V. J. (1999), Interview, 'Revisiting bodies and pleasures', *Theory Culture & Society*, 16 (2), 11–20.

(2000a), *Antigone's Claim: Kinship between Life and Death* (New York: Columbia University Press).

and Laclau, E. and Žižek, S. (2000b), *Contingency, Hegemony, Universality: Contemporary Dialogues on the Left* (London and New York: Verso).

(2000), 'Agencies of style for a liminal subject', in P. Gilroy, L. Grossberg and A. McRobbie (eds), *Without Guarantees: In Honour of Stuart Hall* (London and New York: Verso), 30–7.

(2000), 'Appearances aside', *California Law Review*, 88 (1), 55.

(2000), 'Circuits of bad conscience: Nietzsche and Freud', in A. D. Schrift (ed.), *Why Nietzsche Still? Reflections on Drama, Culture, Politics* (Berkeley, CA: University of California Press), 121–35.

(2000), 'Ethical ambivalence', in M. Garber, B. Hanssen and R. L. Walkowitz (eds), *The Turn to Ethics* (New York and London: Routledge), 15–28.

(2000), 'The force of fantasy: Feminism, Mapplethorpe, and discursive excess', in D. Cornell (ed.), *Feminism and Pornography* (Oxford and New York: Oxford University Press), 487–508.

(2000), 'Longing for recognition: Commentary on the work of Jessica Benjamin', *Studies in Gender and Sexuality*, 1 (3), 271–90.

(2000), 'Subjection, resistance, resignification: Between Freud and Foucault', in W. Brogan and J. Risser (eds), *American Continental Philosophy* (Bloomington and Indianapolis: Indiana University Press), 335–51.

(2000), 'The value of being disturbed', *Theory and Event*, 4 (1), online journal.

and Connolly, W. (2000), 'Politics, power and ethics: A discussion between Judith Butler and William Connolly', *Theory and Event*, 4 (2), online journal.

and Guillory, J. and Thomas, K. (2000), 'Preface', in J. Butler, J. Guillory and K. Thomas (eds), *What's Left of Theory? New Work on the Politics of Literary Theory* (New York: Routledge), viii–xii.

and Olson, G. and Worsham, L. (2000), Interview. 'Changing the subject: Judith Butler's politics of radical resignification', *jac*. 20 (4), 727–65.

(2001), 'Can the other to philosophy speak', in D. Keates and J. W. Scott (eds), *Schools of Thought: Twenty-Five Years of Interpretative Social Science* (Institute for Advance Study, Princeton, NJ: Princeton University Press), 52–66.

(2001), 'Conversational break: A reply to Robert Gooding-Williams', in R. Bernasconi (ed.), *Race: Blackwell Readings in Continental Philosophy* (Oxford: Blackwell), 260–5.

(2001), 'Doing justice to someone: Sex reassignment and allegories of transexuality', *GLQ*, 7 (4), 621–36.

(2001), 'The end of sexual difference?', in E. Bronfen and M. Kavka (eds), *Feminist Consequences: Theory for the New Century* (New York: Columbia University Press), 414–34.

(2001), 'Giving an account of oneself', *Diacritics*, 31 (4), 22–40.

(2001), 'How can I deny that these hands and this body are mine?', in T. Cohen, B. Cohen, J. Hillis Miller and A. Warminski (eds), *Material Events: Paul de Man and the Afterlife of Theory* (Minneapolis: University of Minnesota Press), 254–76.

(2001), 'Sexual difference as a question of ethics', in L. Doyle (ed.), *Bodies of Resistance* (Evanston, IL: Northwestern University Press), 59–77.

(2001), 'There is a person here', Interview, *International Journal of Sexuality and Gender Studies*, 1–2, 7–23.

(2001), 'Withholding the name: Gender as translation in Willa Cather's "On the Gull's Road"', in H. Stevens (ed.), *Modernist Sexualities: Gender and Modernity* (Cambridge, UK: Cambridge University Press), 56–71.

and Paul Rabinow (2001), 'Dialogue: *Antigone*, speech, performance, power', in S. I. Salamensky (ed.), *Talk, Talk, Talk: The Cultural Life of Everyday Conversation* (New York: Routledge), 37–48.

(2002), 'Afterword', in S. Felman, *The Scandal of the Speaking Body* (Stanford, CA: Stanford University Press), 113–23.

(2002), 'Capacity', in S. Barber and D. Clark (eds), *Regarding Sedgwick: Essays on Critical Theory and Queer Culture* (New York: Routledge), 109–19).

(2002), 'Dehumanization via indefinite detention', in D. Goldberg (ed.), *It's a Free Country: Personal Freedom in America after 9/11* (New York: RMD Press), 265–79.

(2002), 'Doubting love', in J. Harmon (ed.), *Take My Advice: Letters to the Next Generation from People Who Know a Thing or Two* (New York: Simon and Schuster), 62–6.

(2002), 'Explanation and exoneration, or what we can hear', *Theory and Event*, 5 (4), online journal; reprinted in *Grey Room* 07, a special issue on 9/11, Spring 2002, 56-67.

(2002), 'Guantánamo limbo: International law offers too little protection for prisoners of the new war', *Nation*, 274 (12), 20–4.

(2002), 'Is kinship always already heterosexual?', in *differences: A Journal of Feminist Cultural Studies*, 13 (1), 14–44.

(2002), Review of J. Goldberg's *Desiring Women Writing: English Renaissance Examples*, *Shakespeare Studies*, 10, 234–42.

and Dolan, F. (eds), (2002), *Atopia: Series on Aesthetic and Political Theory* (Stanford, CA: Stanford University Press).

and Puigvert L. (eds), (2002), *Women and Social Transformation* (New York: Counterpoint).

(2003), 'After loss, what then?', in D. Eng, and D. Kazanjian (eds), *Loss* (California: California University Press), 467–73.

(2003), 'Beauvoir on Sade: Making sexuality into an ethic', in C. Card (ed.), *The Cambridge Companion to Simone de Beauvoir* (Cambridge, UK: Cambridge University Press), 168–88.

(2003), 'No, it's not anti-semitic: Judith Butler defends the right to criticise Israel', *The London Review of Books*, 25 (16), 21 August, 19–21.

(2003), 'Reflections on Germany', in D. Boyarin (ed.), *Queer Theory and the Jewish Question* (New York: Columbia University Press), 395–402.

(2003), 'Values of difficulty', in J. Culler and K. Lamb (eds), *Just Being Difficult? Academic Writing in the Public Arena* (Stanford, CA: Stanford University Press), 199–215.

(2003), 'Violence, mourning, politics', *Studies in Gender and Sexuality*, 4 (1), 9–37.

(2004a), *Undoing Gender* (New York: Routledge).

and Salih, S. (ed.), (2004b), *The Judith Butler Reader* (London: Basil Blackwell).

(2004c), 'What is critique? An essay on Foucault's virtue', in S. Salih (ed.), *The Judith Butler Reader* (London: Basil Blackwell), 302–22; (orig. 2001), in D. Ingram (ed.), *The Political: Readings in Continental Philosophy* (London, Basil Blackwell).

(2004), 'Jacques Derrida', *The London Review of Books*, 26 (21), 4 November, 32.

(2004), 'Performativity', in J. Wolfreys (ed.), *Critical Keywords in Literary and Cultural Theory* (New York/Hampshire: Palgrave Macmillan), 182–9.

(2004), *Precarious Life: Powers of Violence and Mourning* (London: Verso).

(2004), 'Surface tensions: Diane Arbus', *Artforum*, 42 (6), 119.

(2005), *Giving an Account of Oneself* (New York: Fordham University Press).

(2005), 'Jacques Derrida: Affirm the survival', in *Radical Philosophy*, 129, Jan/Feb, 22–5.

(2005), 'Photography, war, outrage', *PMLA*, 120 (3), 822–8.

Forthcoming

'Academic norms, contemporary challenges: A response to Robert Post on academic freedom', in B. Doumani (ed.), *Academic Freedom after September 11th* (Paris/New York: Zone Books).

'Afterword', in E. T. Armour and S. M. St. Ville (eds), *Bodily Citations: Religion and Judith Butler* (Chicago: University of Chicago Press).

'The charge of anti-Semitism: Jews, Israel, and the risk of public critique', in T. Kushner and A. Solomon (eds.), *Wrestling with Zion: Writings by Progressive Jews* (Grove Press).

'The desire to live: Spinoza's ethics under pressure', in V. Kahn and N. Saccamano (eds.), *Politics and Passions* (Princeton University Press).

'Hegel', Encyclopaedia entry in L. Kritzman (ed.), *Twentieth Century French Thought* (New York: Columbia University Press).

'Introduction', in G. Lukacs, *Soul and Form* (New York Review of Books).

'Merleau-Ponty and the touch of Malebranche', in T. Carmen (ed.), *Merleau-Ponty Reader* (Cambridge, UK: Cambridge University Press).

'Regulation', in G. Herdt and C. Stimpson (eds.), *Critical Terms in Gender Studies* (Chicago: University of Chicago Press).

'Sexual difference as a question of ethics', in L. Doyle (ed.), *Political Phenomenologies*.

'Shadows of Algiers: Sartre and Fanon on the question of violence', in J. Judaken (ed.), *Race After Sartre*.

'Torture and the ethics of photography', in an expanded version of *Precarious Life*.

'Undiagnosing gender', in P. Currah and S. Minter (eds), *Transgender Rights: Culture, Politics and Law* (University of Minnesota Press).

'Violence, non-violence: Benjamin's critique of violence', *Aesthetics and Ethics*, with Tate Museum of Modern Art, in conjunction with Basil Blackwell/Routledge.

Other works cited

Althusser, L. (1971), 'Ideology and ideological state apparatuses (notes towards an investigation)', in *Lenin and Philosophy*, trans. B. Brewster (New York and London: Monthly Review Press).

Austin, J. L. (1975), *How To Do Things with Words* (Cambridge, MA: Harvard University Press).

Barad, K. (forthcoming), *Meeting the Universe Halfway* (Durham and London: Duke University Press).

Bennett, A. (2001), 'Re-cognising power: A discourse analysis of power relations', unpublished doctoral thesis, University of New South Wales, Sydney.

Benveniste, E. (1971), *Problems in General Linguistics*, trans. M. E. Meek (Coral Gables Florida: University of Miami Press).

Borch-Jacobsen, M. (1999), *The Freudian Subject*, trans. C. Porter (Stanford, CA: Stanford University Press).

Bordo, S. (1993), *Unbearable Weight: Feminism, Western Culture, and the Body* (Berkeley, CA: California University Press).

Campbell, K. (2005), 'The plague of the subject: Psychoanalysis and Judith Butler's *Psychic Life of Power*', in *Judith Butler: Ten Years After Gender Trouble*, (M. Soenser Breen and W. S. Blumenfield ed. (Hampshire: Ashgate), pp. 81–94.

Cheah, P. (1996), 'Mattering', *Diacritics*, 26 (1), 108–39.

Derrida, J. (1970), 'Scribble (writing/power)', *Yale French Studies*, 58, 116–47.

Derrida, J. (1984), *Of Grammatology*, trans. G. Chakravorty Spivak (Baltimore, MD and London: Johns Hopkins University Press).

Derrida, J. (1985), 'From restricted to general economy: A Hegelianism without reserve', in *Writing and Difference*, trans. A. Bass (London, Melbourne and Henley: Routledge and Kegan Paul).

Derrida, J. (1988a), 'Signature event context', in *Limited Inc.*, trans. S. Weber and J. Mehlman, ed. G. Graff (Evanston, IL: Northwestern University Press).

Derrida, J. (1988b), 'Afterword: Toward an ethic of discussion', in *Limited Inc.*, trans. S. Weber and J. Mehlman, ed. G. Graff (Evanston, IL: Northwestern University Press).

Descombes, V. (1982), *Modern French Philosophy*, trans. J. M. Harding (Cambridge, UK: Cambridge University Press).

Dollimore, J. (1996), 'Bisexuality, heterosexuality, and wishful theory', *Textual Practice*, 10 (3), 523–39.

Foucault, M. (1979), 'Governmentality', trans. Pasquale Pasquino, *Ideology and Consciousness*, 6, 5–21.

Foucault, M. (1980a), *The History of Sexuality, Volume I: An Introduction*, trans. Robert Hurley (New York: Vintage Books, Random House).

Foucault, M. (1980b), 'The confession of the flesh', in *Power/Knowledge: Selected Interviews and Other Writings 1972–1977*, trans. Colin Gordon, Leo Marshall, John Mepham, Kate Soper, ed. Colin Gordon (Brighton, Sussex: The Harvester Press).

Foucault, M. (ed.) (1980c), *Herculine Barbin, Being the Recently Discovered Memoirs of a Nineteenth Century Hermaphrodite*, trans. Richard McDougall (New York: Colophon).

Foucault, M. (1982), *Discipline and Punish: The Birth of the Prison*, trans. A. Sheridan (Harmondsworth, Middlesex: Penguin Books).

Foucault, M. (1984), 'Nietzsche, genealogy, history', in *The Foucault Reader*, trans. D. F. Bouchard and S. Simon, ed. P. Rabinow (New York: Pantheon), 76–100.

Foucault, M. (1986), *The Use of Pleasure: History of Sexuality, Volume 2*, trans. Robert Hurley (New York: Vintage Books, Random House).

Fraser, N. (1997a), *Justice Interruptus: Critical Reflections on the 'Postsocialist' Condition* (New York: Routledge).

Fraser, N. (1997), 'Heterosexism, misrecognition and capitalism: A response to Judith Butler', *Social Text*, 52/3, 279–89.

Freud, S. (1960), 'The ego and the super-ego (ego-ideal)', in *The Ego and The Id*, trans. Joan Riviere, ed. James Strachey (New York: Norton).

Freud, S. (1976), 'Mourning and melancholia', in *General Psychological Theory*, ed. Philip Rieff (New York: Macmillan).

Freud, S. (1991a), 'On narcissism, an introduction', *The Pelican Freud Library*, 11 (London: Penguin), 59–97.

Freud, S. (1991b), 'The ego and the id', *The Pelican Freud Library*, 11 (London: Penguin), 339–407.

Hegel, G. W. F. (1807/1977), *Phenomenology of Spirit*, trans. A. V. Miller (Oxford: Oxford University Press).

Hoffmeyer, J. (1996), *Signs of Meaning in the Universe*, trans. B. J. Haveland (Bloomington, IN: Indiana University Press).

Hood-Williams, J. and Cealey Harrison, W. (1998), 'Trouble with gender', *The Sociological Review*, 46 (1), 73–94.

Hyppolite, J. (1974), *Genesis and Structure of Hegel's 'Phenomenology of Spirit'*, trans. Samuel Cherniak and John Heckman (Evanston, IL: Northwestern University Press).

Irigaray, L. (1985a), *Speculum of the Other Woman*, trans. G. C. Gill (Ithaca, NY: Cornell University Press).

Irigaray, L. (1985b), *This Sex Which Is Not One*, trans. Catherine Porter with Carolyn Burke (Ithaca, NY: Cornell University Press).

Kirby, V. (1997), *Telling Flesh: The Substance of the Corporeal* (New York and London: Routledge).

Kojève, A. (1980), *Introduction to the Reading of Hegel*, trans. James H. Nichols, A. Bloom (ed.) (Ithaca, NY: Cornell University Press).

Kristeva, J. (1980), *Desire in Language: A Semiotic Approach to Literature and Art*, trans. Thomas Gorz, Alice Jardine and Leon S. Roudiez, ed. Leon S. Roudiez (New York: Columbia University Press).

Kristeva, J. (1984), *Revolution in Poetic Language*, trans. Margaret Walker (New York: Columbia University Press).

Lacan, J. (1977a), 'The mirror stage as formative of the function of the I as revealed in psychoanalytic experience', in *Écrits: A Selection* (London: Routledge), 1–7.

Lacan, J. (1977b), 'The signification of the phallus', in *Écrits: A Selection* (London: Routledge), 281–91.

Langton, R. (Fall 1993), 'Speech acts and unspeakable acts', *Philosophy and Public Affairs*, 22 (4), 293–330.

Laplanche, J. and Pontalis, J.-B. (1973), *The Language of Psychoanalysis*, trans. Donald Nicholson-Smith (New York and London: Norton).

Lévi-Strauss, C. (1968), *Structural Anthropology*, trans. Claire Jacobson and Brooke Grundfest Schoepf (London: Allen Lane).

Lévi-Strauss, C. (1969), *The Elementary Structures of Kinship*, trans. James Harle Bell, John Richard Von Sturmer and Rodney Needham (Boston, MA: Beacon Press).

Lloyd, G. (1993), *The Man of Reason: 'Male' and 'Female' in Western Philosophy* (London: Routledge).

Macherey, P. (1992), 'Towards a natural history of norms', in *Michel Foucault Philosopher* (New York: Routledge).

MacKinnon, C. (1993), *Only Words* (Cambridge, MA: Harvard University Press).

Matsuda, M. J., Lawrence III, C. R., Delgado, R. and Crenshaw, K. W. (1993), *Words that Wound: Critical Race Theory, Assaultive Speech, and the First Amendment* (Boulder, CO: Westview Press).

McNay, L. (1999), 'Subject, psyche and agency: The work of Judith Butler', *Theory, Culture & Society*, 16 (2), 175–93.

Mills, C. (2003), 'Contesting the political: Butler and Foucault on power and resistance', *The Journal of Political Philosophy*, 11 (3), 253–72.

Moller Okin, S. (1979), *Women in Western Political Thought* (Princeton, NJ: Princeton University Press).

Morris, D. B. (1991), *The Culture of Pain* (Berkeley and Los Angeles: University of California Press).

Nancy, J.-L. and Lacoue-Labarthe, P. (1992), *The Title of the Letter: A*

Reading of Lacan, trans. F. Raffoul and D. Pettigrew (Albany, NY: SUNY Press).

Nussbaum, M. (1999), 'The professor of parody', *The New Republic*, 220 (8), Feb. 22, 1–13, http://www.tnr.com/index.mhtml.

Rich, A. (1983), 'Compulsory heterosexuality and lesbian existence', in *Powers of Desire: The Politics of Sexuality*, ed. Ann Snitow, Christine Stansell and Sharon Thompson (New York: Monthly Review Press), 177–205.

Riviere, J. (1986), 'Womanliness as a masquerade', in *Formations of Fantasy*, ed. Victor Burgin, James Donald, Cora Kaplan (London: Methuen).

Wilson, E. A. (2004), *Psychosomatic: Feminism and the Neurological Body* (Durham and London: Duke University Press).

Yeghiayan, E. http://sun3.lib.uci.edu/indiv/scctr/Wellek/builder/html7.

Index